# CLASSIC
# IN SUSSEX

BEN PERKINS

**S. B. Publications**

By the same author:

*South Downs: Walks for Motorists*
*Pub Walks in the South Downs*
*Village Walks in East Sussex*
*Waterside Walks in Sussex*
*Sussex Border Path: Guide and Map Pack*
*On Foot on the East Sussex Downs*
*On Foot on the West Sussex Downs*
*On Foot on the Weald*

Contributed walks to:

*Walkers Britain and Walkers Britain 2*
*AA Book of Village Walks*
*Exploring Britain's Long Distance Paths*
*AA Book of Family Walks*

First published in 2001 by S.B. Publications. Tel: 01323 893498
Email: sbpublications@tiscali.co.uk www.sbpublications.co.uk

Reprinted 2007



ISBN 1 85770 223 9
978 185770 2231

Typeset by Design 2 Output, Eastbourne.

Front Cover Photograph by Graham Thornton.

# CONTENTS

# ACKNOWLEDGMENTS

The author is indebted to John Barnes, Brian Ellis, Ron Keen, Ann Lindfield and Roy Marchant, all experienced local ramblers, who have helped him with the difficult task of deciding which areas, features and walks to include in this collection and the even more difficult decisions about some beautiful places and walks which had, reluctantly, to be omitted.

*Front Cover:* River Cuckmere from High and Over (Walk 2)

*Back Cover:* Fairlight Glen (Walk 3)

*Title Page:* Chichester Harbour Path beyond Chalkdock Point (Walk 1)

# INTRODUCTION

What turns a country walk into a classic? Its an overused label, but one of the main Oxford Dictionary definitions is 'of the first rank' and that is not a bad way of describing the walks in this book. They have each been chosen because they offer something special, whether it be the variety and quality of the countryside through which they pass or the uniqueness, beauty or historical associations of the places visited. In the end the choice has to be a fairly subjective one and probably boils down to a selection of personal favourite walks.

With such a richly endowed landscape and 4000 miles of public rights of way to choose from, the problem has been not which walks to include but which to leave out. I have been conscious of the need to spread the walks fairly evenly throughout the two administrative counties of East and West Sussex. However, not surprisingly, the majority of the walks can be found within the two designated Areas of Natural Beauty, the Downs and the High Weald, where much of the best walking is concentrated.

I have grouped the walks geographically, both for ease of reference and also as a reminder of the remarkable variety of landscape to be found within Sussex. Although several tourist 'honey-pots' are included, notably, and I hope justifiably, Devil's Dyke, Alfriston, and the Seven Sisters Country Park, some of the areas explored are much less well known. For beauty and remoteness, try the two walks in the West Sussex Weald, both within the official Downs AONB but much quieter and less frequented than the chalk downland to the south. Even within the Downs it is easy to get away from the crowds such as on Walk 7, deep in rolling hills on the dip slope of the Downs to the north of Chichester.

The walks vary in length between 4 and 12 miles but most of them are of medium length and can be completed during a leisurely half day. All start from a convenient parking area and about half can be accessed using public transport. All are circular except the Chichester Harbour walk which has been designed as a linear stroll beside the water, using a convenient bus service back to the start.

The standard of maintenance of rights of way in both East and West Sussex has steadily improved in recent years and you will find that most of the paths are reasonably well signed or waymarked and in good condition. Some paths can become overgrown, particularly in late summer and mud underfoot may be a problem, particularly in areas of Wealden clay during the winter months. Although you should be able to navigate successfully with only the walk description and sketch map to guide you, I would strongly recommend having a map to hand at all times. Features such as fences, stiles and signs do appear and disappear from year to year. Paths are sometimes legally diverted and if you do happen to go astray, a map is essential. The OS Explorer maps are perfect for the job and now provide additional information in the form of the boundaries of public open access areas such as Ashdown Forest and the Seven Sisters Country Park.

Having sampled some of the walks in this collection I hope you will agree with me that they offer something special, adding up to the *crème de la crème* of this splendid walking area.

*BP*

*South Downs Way from Beacon Hill (Walk 6)*

# LOCATION OF WALKS

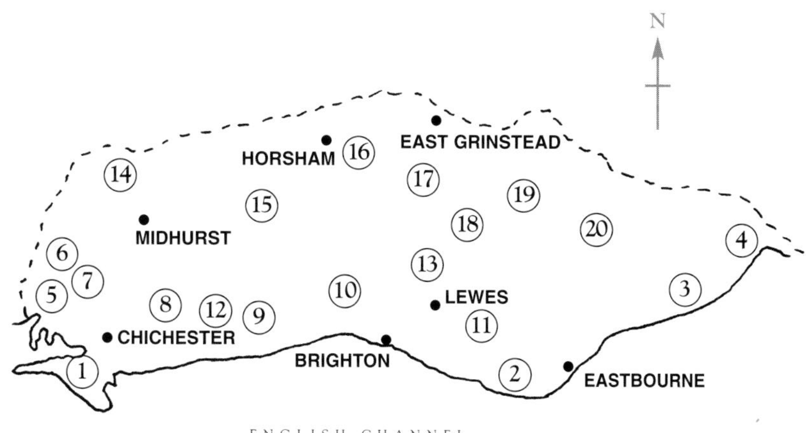


**THE COAST**

1. Chichester Harbour
2. The Seven Sisters and Friston Forest
3. Hastings Country Park
4. Rye, Winchelsea and Camber Castle

**THE DOWNS**

5. Kingley Vale and Stoughton
6. Harting Downs, Beacon Hill and Hooksway
7. Chilgrove and the Mardens
8. Bignor Post, Barlavington and Sutton
9. Chanctonbury and Cissbury Rings
10. Devil's Dyke, Newtimber and Poynings
11. Berwick, Alciston and the East Sussex Downs

**THE RIVER VALLEYS**

12. Burpham and the Arun Valley
13. Barcombe Mills and the River Ouse

**THE WEST SUSSEX WEALD**

14. Blackdown and Fernhurst
15. The Mens and Fittleworth Wood

**THE HIGH WEALD**

16. St.Leonard's Forest
17. Balcombe and Wakehurst
18. Ashdown Forest
19. Mayfield
20. Brightling and Fuller's Follies

## Walk 1
# CHICHESTER HARBOUR

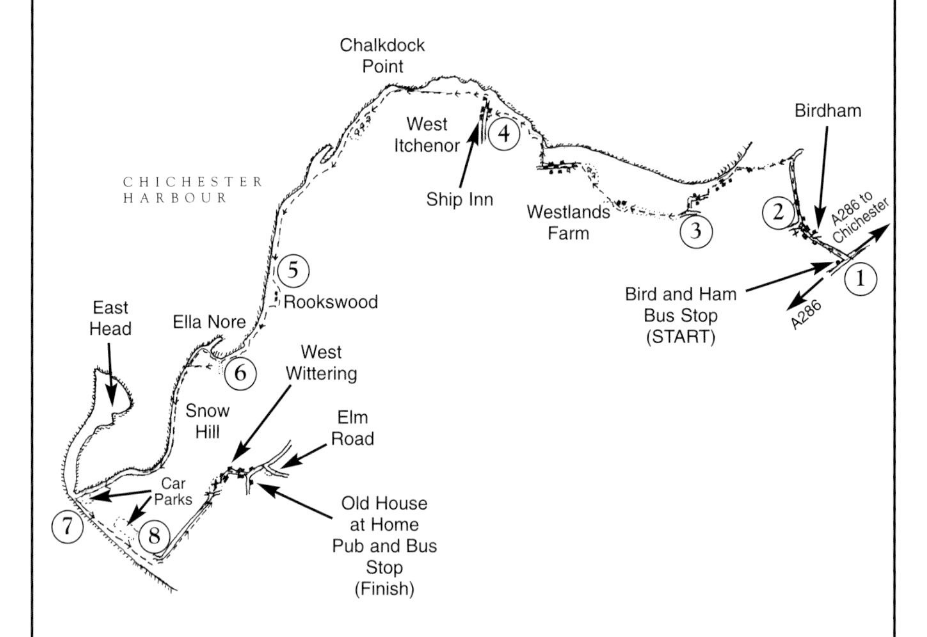

*Birdham Church.*

Walk 1

# CHICHESTER HARBOUR

| | |
|---|---|
| **Distance:** | 7 miles. |
| **Route:** | Birdham – Westlands Farm – West Itchenor – Ella Nore – East Head – West Wittering (Linear). |
| **Map:** | OS Explorer 120: Chichester. |
| **PublicTransport:** | bus from Chichester to the Bird and Ham Pub bus stop (though there is no pub now) at the junction of the A286 with Church Lane, Birdham (GR 827000) where the walk description starts. Bus back from West Wittering. Hourly weekday service in each direction, two hourly on Sundays. |
| **Start/Parking:** | if arriving by car, park to the north of Birdham Church (GR 823003) joining the walk at point 2 and catching a bus back from West Wittering, alighting at the Bird and Ham. Alternatively, if you prefer to time your bus journey for the start of the day, park at West Wittering and catch a bus from the Old House at Home pub to the Bird and Ham for the start of the walk. Parking is not easy at West Wittering. You should find some roadside parking a few yards along Elm Lane at GR 781985 (see sketch map). |
| **Conditions:** | easy level walking along good paths and tracks. Generally dry underfoot even in winter. |
| **Refreshments:** | Ship Inn at West Itchenor, Old House at Home pub at West Wittering. |

With 50 miles of shoreline, embracing 11 square miles of saltmarsh and mudflat, Chichester Harbour is a haven for wildlife, notably nesting birds in the spring and vast flocks of migrant birds in the autumn and winter. Winter is also the best time to enjoy this walk when the equally vast hordes of tourists who descend upon West Wittering in the summer are gone.

This is the only walk in the book which is not circular. This allows us, wherever public rights of way permit, to follow the edge of the harbour for much of the walk. It also avoids the need for a less interesting return route along inland field paths. If you have a map, such a route is quite feasible, as I found when planning the walk for this book, but the full circuit would add up to about 12 miles in all. Details of how to combine walk and bus are included in the fact file (page 9).

# THE WALK

*From the Bird in Ham Pub bus stop, (a misleading name since the pub is long gone), start the walk from the A286 along Church Lane* **(1)**. *Follow the lane to reach the small triangular village green by Birdham church* **(2)**. *Join the walk here if you have parked by the church.*

This is a pleasant spot. A small commemorative plaque on the green bears the appropriate legend 'If you want a memorial, look around.'

*Go ahead along a lane, leaving the green on your left. It is signed as a private road to Court Farm, but also as a public footpath. After another quarter of a mile fork left along the drive to a house called 'Harbour Meadow'. Just short of the house entrance fork left along a field headland path. A path continues along the edge of the harbour, squeezed between the water and some large gardens and then turns inland where you should join and bear right along an estate road.*

*At a T-junction with a lane* **(3)**, *turn right. After a few yards, ignoring a signed path to the left, go ahead along the concrete drive to Westlands Farm. About 100 yards short of the buildings, fork left along a path which diverts to the left of the house and garden (not the Saltern way which goes squarely left from this point). Beyond the property fork right with a fence and subsequently a copse on your right.*

*Turn left along an estate drive. Just past Harbour House on your right, turn right along a twitten which takes you out to the edge of the harbour once more. A good path now follows the top of the harbour wall. Just short of a jetty, turn left along an access drive to join a road at West Itchenor opposite the Ship Inn* **(4)**. *Turn right and walk out to the quay.*

West Itchenor is the official point of entry for the harbour and is the only place where boats can be launched whatever the state of the tide. It was once a major shipbuilding centre. A passenger ferry operates across the main channel to the Bosham peninsula during the summer months (weekends from April to September, daily from mid-July to mid-September).

*Just past the Harbour Office on your left, turn left along a narrow gravel path. Go straight ahead through a boat yard and on along a clear path, passing a sheltered harbour viewpoint on the right.*

At Chalkdock Point the area on your left was reclaimed for grazing in the last century. A tidal flap in the harbour wall allowed fresh water out but prevented salt water getting in. The area is now being allowed to revert to saltmarsh.

*A delightful path continues through a small copse of mixed oak and beech and on past more gnarled and ancient oak trees which have, amazingly, survived the combined battering of wind and tidal erosion. The path opens out to follow the harbour wall with wide views across the main channel to the Bosham Peninsula. At Rookswood* **(5)** *the path briefly diverts inland to get round another group of houses, following an estate road for a short distance before returning to the edge of the harbour.*

*At Ella Nore* **(6)** *a lane provides a direct route into West Wittering but the full walk continues beside the harbour. A little further on a signed path to the right indicates a pleasant short detour, except if the tide is very high, out on to a shingle spit, returning to rejoin the main path along the top of the shingle bank.*

Look out for Sea Campion, Sea Kale and Yellow Horned Poppy which manage to thrive on this inhospitable shingle habitat.

*Where the path opens out at a large grassy area, continue ahead along the water's edge and on along the sea wall with the sandy spit of East Head in view across the water to your right.*

On your left are the mud flats and salt marsh of Snow Hill, partially covered at high tide and an excellent place for bird watching. When the tide is low look out for wading birds such as Curlew, Dunlin and Redshank.

*On reaching the large car park at the harbour entrance* **(7)**, *you have an opportunity to detour to the right along the fragile sandy spit of East Head, adding a mile to the length of the walk. To complete the described walk turn left beside the sea, walking either along the raised shingle bank, or, at low tide, along the beach. You will be passing through an area of beach huts, best enjoyed in the deserted winter months. After about half a mile* **(8)**, *on approaching the first solid dwellings, turn inland to follow a path beside the access road from the beach car parks, now heading for West Wittering Church. At a road junction go straight ahead through the churchyard. Leave through the main church gate and go ahead along a lane which takes you to a junction with the B2179. The stop for the bus back to Birdham is now a few yards to the right by the Old House at Home pub.*

Chichester Harbour Path beyond Chaldock Point.

Walk 2

# THE SEVEN SISTERS AND FRISTON FOREST

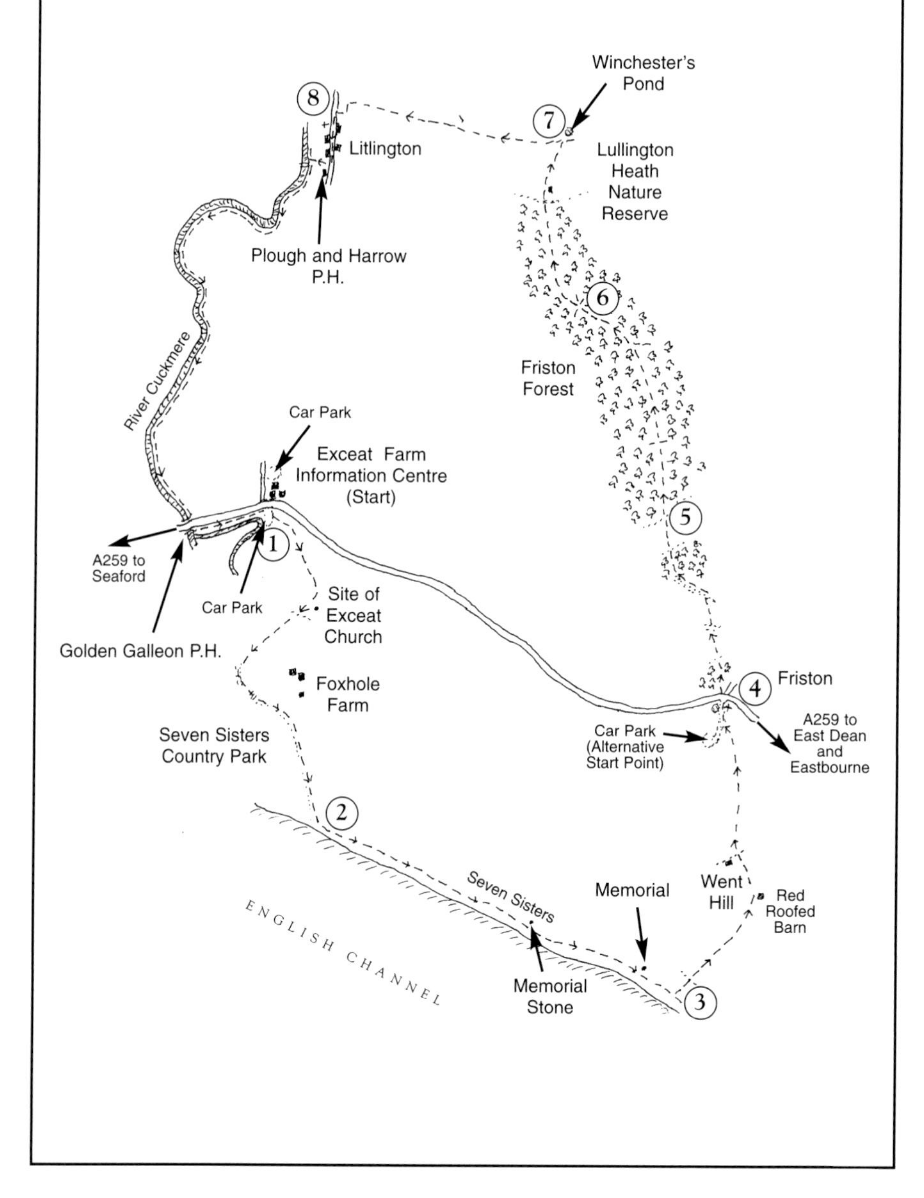

# Walk 2
# THE SEVEN SISTERS AND FRISTON FOREST

| | |
|---|---|
| **Distance:** | 11 miles. |
| **Route:** | Exceat Car Park – Exceat Hill – Foxhole Bottom – Seven Sisters – Went Hill – Friston – Friston Forest – Winchester's Pond – Litlington – Cuckmere River Bank – Exceat. |
| **Map:** | OS Explorer 123: South Downs Way – Newhaven to Eastbourne. |
| **Start/Parking:** | at Exceat on the A259 road between Seaford and Eastbourne. There are two car parks, one on the south side of the road and the other behind the Seven Sisters Country Park information centre (GR 518995). Fee payable. |
| **Public Transport:** | reasonably frequent bus service from Seaford or Eastbourne. |
| **Conditions:** | a fairly hilly and strenuous walk, but all on good paths and tracks, except for the possibility of some mud underfoot in Friston Forest. |
| **Refreshments:** | Plough and Harrow pub at Litlington, Golden Galleon pub at Exceat Bridge. |

This longish circuit embraces some of the very best walking in the Sussex Downs. It starts across open downland, part of the Seven Sisters Country Park, taking us out to the edge of the precipitous chalk cliffs on the east side of Cuckmere Haven on the summit of the first of the Seven Sisters. It then follows an exhilarating switch-back route along all seven of the Sisters before turning inland across a large area of open National Trust Land at Crowlink. The walk passes close to Friston Church and Pond before heading north across the rolling beech-wooded downland of Friston Forest before climbing steadily up to a magnificent viewpoint next to Winchester's Pond and the Lullington Heath National Nature Reserve.

A steady descent takes us down onto the Cuckmere valley at Litlington where there is a welcome pub. The last two miles follow the bank of the Cuckmere River back to Exceat and another good pub serving an extensive range of food and good beer.

# THE WALK

*To orientate yourself for the walk, stand at the entrance to the car park on the seaward side of the A259 with your back to the road* **(1)**. *Go left through a gate and fork left. After a few yards, on reaching a concrete drive, go ahead signposted as both South Downs Way and Park Trail. A terraced grassy path climbs, running parallel to the A259 at first. About half way up the hill, where the path divides, keep right along the lower of the two paths, which climbs to contour round the right shoulder of Exceat Hill.*

To the left of the path, at the highest point, a stone plinth marks the site of Exceat Church which stood here between the 13th and 15th Centuries, after which it fell into disuse and finally disappeared.

*Beyond a gate the way posted South Downs Way drops down into Foxhole Bottom where you should go forward along a track for a 50 yards before forking left to a gate and steps. At the top of the steps, ignoring a gate, climb steadily up with a fence on your right. Follow this fence out to the cliff edge on the top of the first of the Seven Sisters* **(2)**.

*Turn left and follow the continually undulating path over all of the Seven Sisters. On the top of the fourth Sister you will enter the National Trust area of Crowlink and on the fifth, pass a memorial stone commemorating the purchase of the area for public enjoyment. The sixth of the Sisters has a notch in it which doesn't count towards the total of seven.*

In Michel Dene between the sixth and the seventh Sister there is a small

*Seven Sisters looking East towards Belle Tout.*

monument to two soldiers who died during World War I and in whose memory the area was donated to the National Trust.

*On the top of the seventh Sister* **(3)**, *just before the path begins to drop down towards Birling Gap, turn left and head inland. Go over a stile on the skyline and continue in the same direction heading for the highest point on Went Hill (there is no defined path but you are crossing open access land). Towards the top, join and follow a faint unfenced track which passes about 100 yards to the left of a red-roofed barn.*

*Beyond the barn veer left round the head of a combe to a swing gate on the skyline about 100 yards to the right of another, ruined, barn. Maintain direction across high open downland, through a kissing gate in an intermediate fence and on to join the access drive from a car park (a possible alternative starting point – see sketch map) in the far field corner. Bear right along this drive out to the A259, passing Friston Pond on the left and church on the right.*

Much of the church is Saxon in origin and it has an open timber roof dating from c 1450. It enjoys a lovely setting, high on a hill, opposite the village pond. Only the noisy traffic on the A259 mars the tranquil scene.

*Cross the main road* **(4)** *and a triangle of grass opposite. Go over a slip road and follow a path which passes through a bridle gate to enter woodland. Once through the gate, turn right and follow a path which drops down, skirting to the left of a covered reservoir, through woodland and then across a large field. Cross a walled drive and continue down across a second field.*

*Exceat Farm from Exceat Hill.*

*On the other side of this field turn left along a path which runs parallel and to the right of another drive at first before climbing steeply up through woodland where you should ignore all crossing tracks. Emerge from the wood and continue in the same direction up across a wide expanse of open downland before re-entering the main bulk of Friston Forest* **(5)**.

*Follow a clear forest track down into a valley and up again, ignoring all side and crossing tracks. The path climbs over Snap Hill. Just beyond the summit, go straight over a crossing bridle way and drop fairly steeply down into the next valley, signposted to The Long Man. Ignoring a signed path to the left, continue down to the bottom of the hill and a point where a number of ways diverge* **(6)**. *Go left and immediately right, then keep right, still signed to The Long Man.*

*A firm well graded track climbs steadily up out of the valley where a clear felled and replanted area opens out to the right. Where the track begins to level out, go ahead, passing on your right a Lullington Heath Nature Reserve notice and a fenced enclosure protecting a borehole and air pollution measurement station.*

The Nature Reserve is a rare local example of chalk heath where plants which thrive in acid and alkaline soils can grow in close proximity.

*At the next path junction fork left and, after a few yards, with another Nature Reserve notice and a flint-enclosed donations box on your right* **(7)**, *bear left again.*

A few yards to the right from this point is Winchester's Pond, once hidden by scrub but recently opened up. This dewpond dates from the last century but was restored in 1979.

*As the track begins to drop down, a superb view opens out across the village of Alfriston and the downs beyond with the distinctive profile of Firle Beacon easily recognisable. At a junction of tracks, go straight ahead, signposted to Litlington. Follow it down into the valley where it veers left and right between farm buildings and out to the lane at Litlington* **(8)**.

*Turn left along the lane passing the 12th to 14th Century church on the right and Litlington Nursery and Tea Gardens on the left. A few yards short of the Plough and Harrow pub turn right along a tarmac twitten, signposted as the South Downs Way. On reaching the Cuckmere River turn left along the raised river bank and follow it for two miles downstream to Exceat Bridge, meandering along the foot of High and Over, rising steeply on the west side of the Cuckmere valley.*

The white horse carved out of the chalk, high on the hillside, is not an ancient hill figure but a relatively modern artefact.

*At Exceat Bridge, where the large and bustling Golden Galleon pub is well placed on the other side of the river, you should turn left beside the A259 walking along a raised path to the right of this busy road. Follow it for a quarter of a mile back to the start.*

*Looking west along the Seven Sisters towards Cuckmere Haven and Seaford Head*

*Alfriston and Firle Beacon*

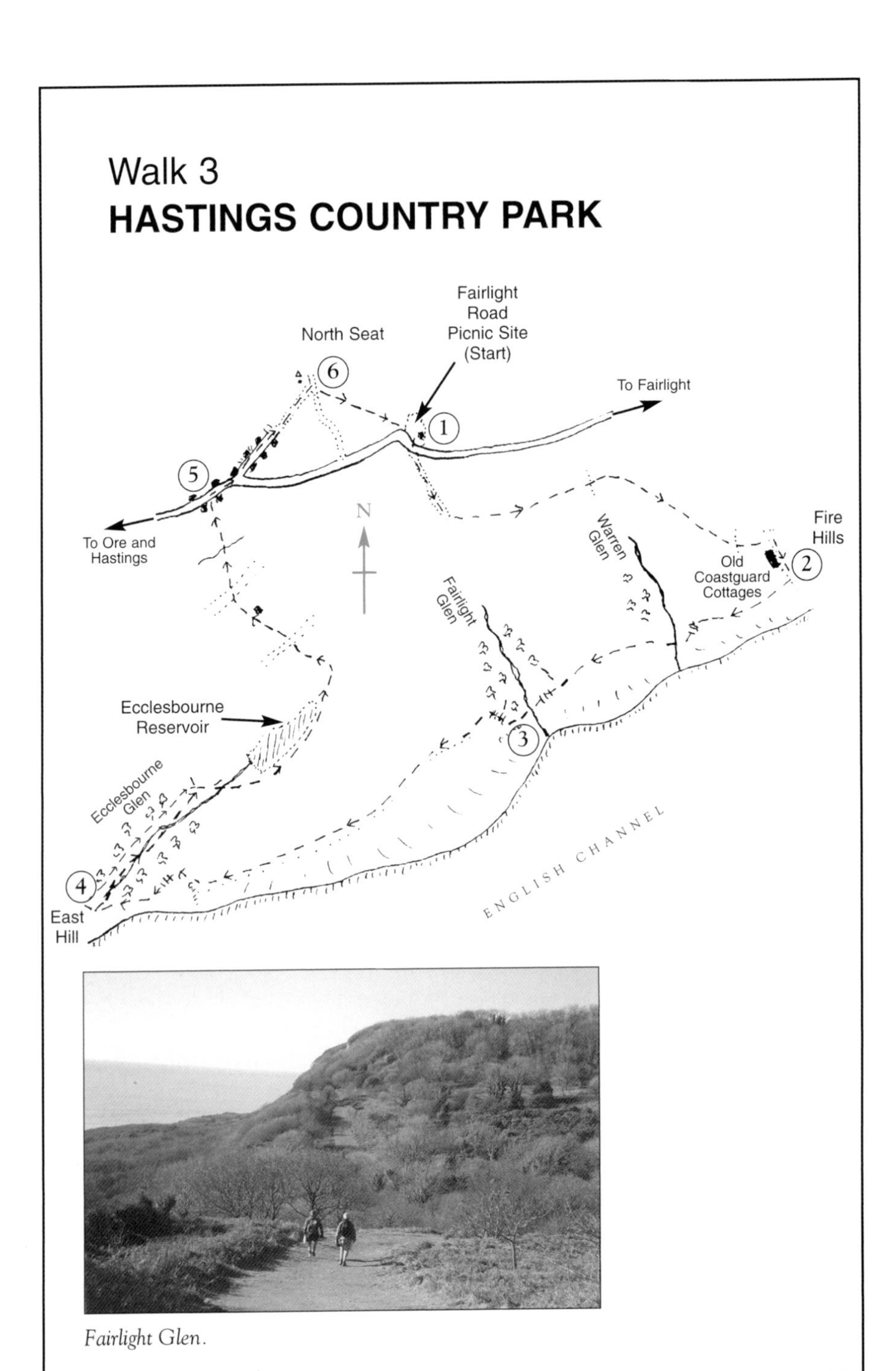


*Fairlight Glen.*

Walk 3

# HASTINGS COUNTRY PARK

| | |
|---|---|
| **Distance:** | 5 miles. |
| **Route:** | Fairlight Road Car Park and Picnic Site – Warren Glen – Fairlight Glen – Ecclesbourne Glen – North Seat – Fairlight Road Car Park. |
| **Map:** | OS Explorer 124: Hastings and Bexhill. |
| **Start/Parking:** | at the Fairlight Road Picnic Site on the Ore-to-Fairlight Cove road about a mile east of Hastings (GR 848118). |
| **Public Transport:** | two-hourly weekday bus service from Hastings. |
| **Conditions:** | a fairly strenuous walk, involving three steep climbs, all on excellent well maintained paths, apart from a few mud patches. |
| **Refreshments:** | none. |

Immediately to the east of Hastings, the Country Park embraces an area of over 600 acres. It is a landscape, unique in Sussex, incorporating three miles of spectacular coastline and three deep wooded glens carved by tiny streams. The crumbling cliffs, formed from ancient sandstone rock, are rich in fossils. Landslips and the constant battering of the sea, have led to steady erosion and loss of sections of the original coastal path. An excellent alternative has been provided, offering an exhilarating switchback walk with well engineered steps to help you up and down the steepest bits. Although only about five miles in length you should allow plenty of time to recover from the steep ascents and enjoy the magnificent scenery. The return route heads inland to visit North Seat, an exceptional viewpoint overlooking Hastings.

# THE WALK

*From the entrance to the car park* **(1)** *cross the Hastings-Fairlight road and follow a tarmac track, opposite, signposted as a footpath to Fairlight Glen. After about 300 yards turn left along a path, enclosed at first, signed to Warren Glen. Go through a swing gate across a shallow dip to a second swing gate and on past a large notice 'Warren Glen'. A wide path contours round the upper end of Warren Glen with a fine view down the glen towards the sea. A gravel path with a metalled access drive, heading for the sea and passing the Old Coastguard Cottages and the modern coastguard station on your right.*

Over to your left is the extensive area of cliff top known as the Fire Hills, offering fine open walking and a magnificent view along the coast towards Dungeness. It is a delightful mix of close-cropped grass interspersed with patches of gorse, heather and bracken. Although not included in this walk it is well worth a detour if time permits. The name may derive from the colour of the gorse in bloom or relate to a time when the gorse was set alight at intervals as a warning to sailors or smugglers.

*Beyond the coastguard enclosure* **(2)** *bear right to a swing gate and the first of a number of solid wooden bollards which you will be meeting at intervals on the coastal walk. This one is numbered 14. A substantial path begins to drop down into Warren Glen. Go left down a flight of steps, across a culverted stream at the bottom and directly ahead on a wide grassy strip which takes you steeply up the other side of the glen.*

*At the top of the steepest part of the slope ignore a path to the right and go ahead to Bollard 13 where you should bear half right up an elaborate flight of steps within a belt of woodland. A path continues across high open cliff top before dropping down another flight of steps into Fairlight Glen. At a T-junction at the foot of the steps, turn left towards the sea. At the bottom of the hill cross a stream* **(3)***.*

Fairlight Glen is thickly wooded, much of it ancient, allowing a variety of wild flowers to thrive, including wood anemone, bluebell and wild garlic.

*At Bollard 10 bear left and right with the main path, climbing steeply once more. Ascend more steps ignoring a path to the right at Bollard 8. At Bollard 7 keep left.*

At the top, to your left, was once the site of Lovers' Seat, a projecting sandstone slab and a superb viewpoint which has now collapsed due to the relentless cliff erosion. It has been estimated that over a metre of coast line is lost each year.

*The walk continues across high ground with views now opening out ahead towards Hastings and westwards along the coast as far as Eastbourne and Beachy Head. At the next bollard, fork left, signed to Ecclesbourne Glen (lower). A few yards before the point where further progress along the cliff is barred by a fence and the edge of the glen, bear right on a path which burrows through scrub, soon dropping down steeply into Ecclesbourne Glen and then up more steps.*

*About half way up the hill* **(4)***, turn right along a path which takes an undulating route along the side of the glen before crossing the stream and climbing steeply.*

Ecclesbourne Glen, the most heavily wooded of the three glens encountered on this walk, provides, in places, a cool and humid micro-climate in which rare ferns and mosses flourish.

*At a T-junction with a wider path turn left and, at a meeting of four ways where you will find Bollard No. 5, go directly ahead signposted to Ecclesbourne Glen (upper). The path now skirts to the right of a reservoir before bearing left across the stream. Join an access drive from a cottage and, after a few yards, go straight across another drive and ahead through a gap, signposted as a footpath to Fairlight Road.*

*Cross a recreation area, passing immediately to the left of a brick toilet block to find the start of a path just to the right of a water tap protected by a low brick wall. A narrow unsigned path goes ahead, burrowing down through a holly thicket, then on across a valley between fences and out to join Fairlight Road* **(5)**.

*Turn right and, after 150 yards, fork left along Beacon Road. Climb steadily. The road becomes an unmade track which takes you up to the high point of North Seat* **(6)**.

Over to your left at the top of the hill is a public access area offering fine views across Hastings and a useful direction indicator plate.

*To complete the walk, just short of a Hastings Country Park map and notice, turn right to a swing gate and along a path through gorse, signposted to Fairlight Road Picnic Site. Ignoring paths to right and left, go ahead across high ground with views northwards for the first time across a wide expanse of the Weald. Follow a fence, right, back to the start.*

*Warren Glen.*

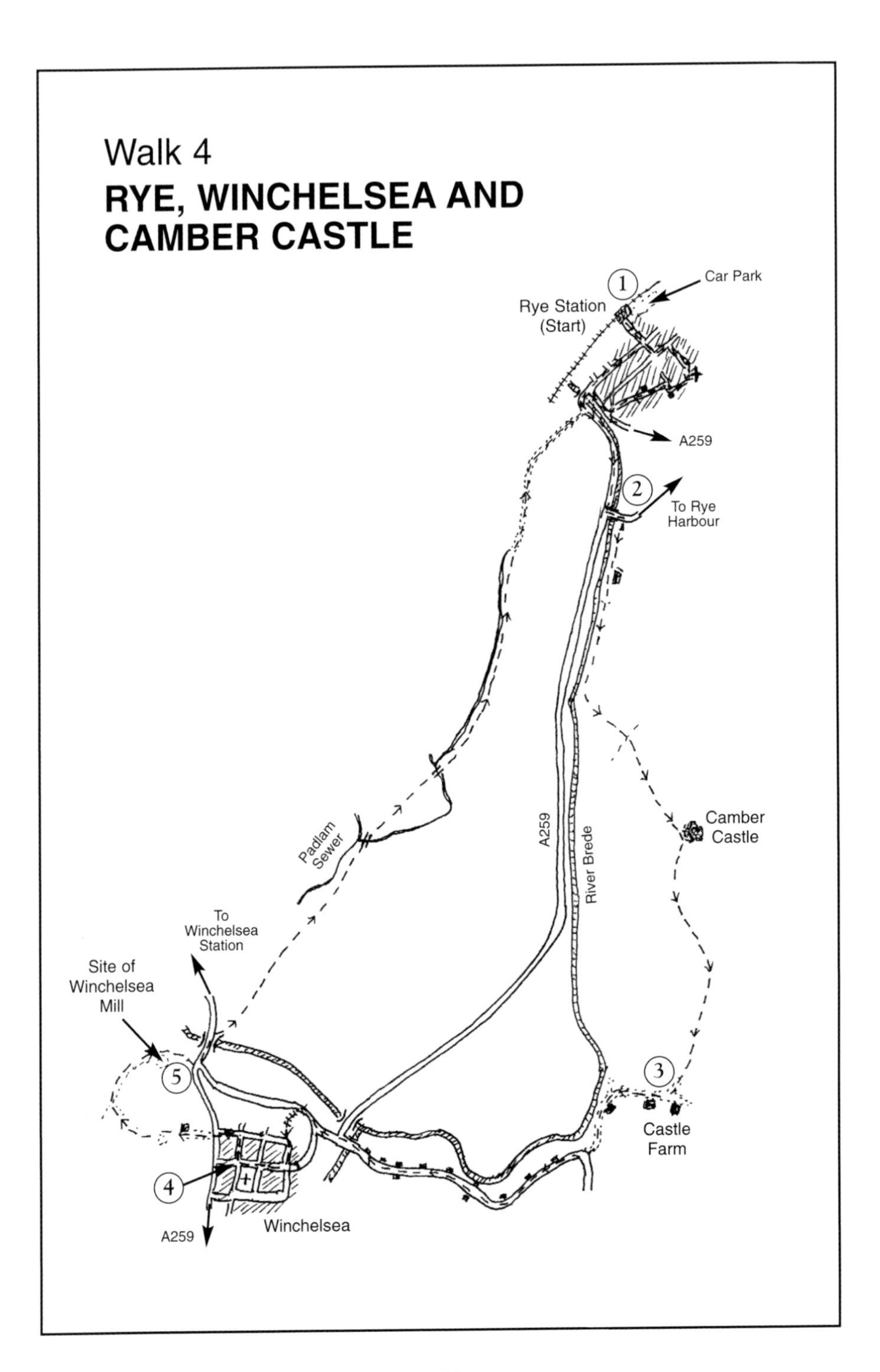
Walk 4
RYE, WINCHELSEA AND CAMBER CASTLE
1
Car Park
Rye Station (Start)
A259
2
To Rye Harbour
A259
River Brede
Padlam Sewer
Camber Castle
To Winchelsea Station
Site of Winchelsea Mill
5
3
Castle Farm
4
A259
Winchelsea

## Walk 4
# RYE, WINCHELSEA AND CAMBER CASTLE

| | |
|---|---|
| **Distance:** | $6^1/_2$ miles. |
| **Route:** | Rye – Camber Castle – Winchelsea – Rye. |
| **Map:** | OS Explorer 125: Romney Marsh, Rye and Winchelsea. |
| **Start/Parking:** | park in the large car park next to Rye Station (fee payable) (GR 919205). |
| **Public Transport:** | train or bus to Rye Station. |
| **Conditions:** | easy walking along field paths and tracks linking the two towns. Cobbled streets in Rye. One short steep climb up into Winchelsea. |
| **Refreshments:** | New Inn at Winchelsea. Numerous pubs in Rye. Tea shops in Winchelsea and Rye. |

Most of this walk crosses featureless drained marshland, once covered by the sea. It would hardly qualify for our 'Top 20' were it not for the fact that it also passes through Rye and Winchelsea, two of the most delightful and historically important small towns in Sussex. Both were admitted to the confederation of Cinque Ports in 1191, conferring financial privileges as well as the duty to maintain a fleet of ships to repel foreign invaders.

The old walled town of Rye stands on a hilltop overlooking the confluence of the River Rother with its two tributaries, the Brede and the Tillingham. The town was raided several times by the French during the Hundred Years War, culminating in a devastating attack in 1377 when most of it was burned to the ground. Rebuilt, it remained a port until the sea receded. The prosperity of the town was bolstered when Queen Elizabeth visited in 1573 and confirmed its royal charter. Many old buildings survive, including the Old Grammar School and the Mermaid Inn, both passed on the walk.

Winchelsea once occupied lower ground, probably on a shingle spit near Camber, some distance away from its present position, but was overwhelmed by the sea in the 13th century. The new town, designed on a grand scale in a 'chequer-board' pattern, occupies a peninsula overlooking the marshes and was first occupied in about 1292. It was once a substantial walled town with a population of 6000 but is now a quiet backwater, though it still retains its town status with an annually elected mayor. Our route through Winchelsea passes several important historical sites, including the well preserved Strand Gate and adjacent Look-Out, the 14th Century Church of St Thomas and, next to it, Wesley's Tree where John Wesley preached his last open-air sermon in 1790. The Court Hall, opposite the church, once used as the town gaol, now houses a small museum.

## THE WALK

*From the station entrance* **(1)** *go ahead along the station approach road. At a road junction go ahead up* Market Road *to join the High Street and turn left. Opposite the Old Rye Grammar School, a weathered brick building dating from 1636, turn right up Lion Street. At the entrance to the church, turn right along a paved path and, at the corner of the churchyard go ahead along the cobbled West Street.*

On the corner ahead is Lamb House, once the home of the writer Henry James. It is open to view from April to October on Wednesday and Saturday afternoons between 2 and 6.

*At the next junction turn left down* Mermaid Street*, passing the Mermaid Inn on your right. At the bottom of the hill go forward to join the main road by the Town Information Centre and turn right. At a mini-roundabout, go left across the River Tillingham and follow the A259 road round to the left. For some of the way there is now an unofficial alternative path beside the river. After about a quarter of a mile, turn left, signposted to Rye Harbour. Cross the River Brede* **(2)***, another tributary of the Rother, next to a lock, and immediately turn right along a roughly metalled drive beside the river.*

*Where the drive divides, fork right, passing to the right of houses, to a gate and continue along the river bank path. After about a quarter of a mile, at a waypost, turn left through a gate and head in the general direction of Camber Castle. Aim for a gate at first to get through an intermediate fence and then veer right directly towards the castle.*

Camber Castle was built by Henry VIII in the 16th Century for defence of the coastline but quickly abandoned as the sea receded. After extensive and endlessly protracted repair work, Camber Castle is at last safe enough to be opened to the public. For information on access telephone 01732 778000.

*A few yards short of the main entrance to the castle veer half right along a track to a stile beside a gate from which a faint unfenced gravel track continues. At Castle Farm* **(3)** *fork right and follow a farm access drive out to a road where you should bear right (almost directly ahead). Follow this road for half a mile or so out to join the A259.*

Just short of this road junction you will cross the Royal Military Canal, built between 1804 and 1806 as part of the defences against a possible Napoleonic

*Rye Church and Lion Street.*

*Mermaid Street, Rye.*

*Camber Castle.*

invasion. It extends from Hythe in Kent to the foot of the cliffs near Fairlight Cove. It can now be followed on foot using a newly created long distance footpath.

*Bear left along the road past the Bridge Inn on your right. At a junction with the road up into Winchelsea on the left, go straight ahead, still beside the A259. After about 100 yards, go left up a steep flight of steps, protected by a handrail, passing one of the original village wells. On reaching a road, go directly ahead to a cross-roads with the High Street where you should turn right.*

Allow time for a short detour to the left to the Strand Gate, built in the 13th Century. The adjacent Lookout, once used to watch for French raiders, is now a splendid vantage point over Romney Marsh and Rye as well as a long stretch of the coastline to the east towards Dungeness Lighthouse and Power Station. On a very clear day it is possible to see the hills behind Boulogne.

*Follow the main street, passing the post office and tea rooms on your left, then the church, also on your left and the 14th Century Court Hall on your right.*

The church, though a substantial structure, is only a fragment of a much grander building. The small museum in the Court Hall is open from May to September on Tuesdays, Saturdays and Bank Holidays from 10.30 am to 12.30 pm and 2.00 to 5.00 pm and on Sundays from 2.00 to 5.00 pm.

*At a road junction by the New Inn* **(4)** *turn right and take the next turning on the left. Cross the A259 and follow the drive opposite where a sign indicates that you are on part* *of the 1066 Country Walk. Where the drive ends go forward across grass to reach a trig point on a grassy mound.*

This is the site of a former windmill which was destroyed during the Great Gale of 1987. Only the foundations now remain. It is a grand viewpoint overlooking the valley of the River Brede.

*The path skirts to the right of the mill site to a gate and then bears right, dropping down, soon between low grassy banks. Towards the bottom of the hill go over a stile and keep right along the foot of a wooded bank. In the field corner go right over a footbridge and follow a well-trodden path which takes you out to the A259 on a hairpin bend* **(5)**.

*Turn left and immediately left again along a lane, signposted to Winchelsea Station and Udimore. Just after crossing a bridge over the River Brede, turn right on a path which crosses a field corner and then veers half left across the next field now aiming more or less directly for Rye. A path is normally trodden out through any growing crop. Maintain direction across the next field and on, now with a drainage channel, the Padlam Sewer, on your left. Cross a substantial footbridge over this waterway and follow the direction of an arrow on the bridge across a large area of sheep-grazed pasture, soon on a low bank. Beyond another footbridge you can pick up and follow, on your left, another drainage ditch. The path becomes a fenced track which takes you out to the A259. Turn left, cross the River Tillingham, and at a mini-roundabout, go straight ahead along Wish Street and subsequently Cinque Port Street. At a road junction by the Cinque Port pub turn left back to the station.*

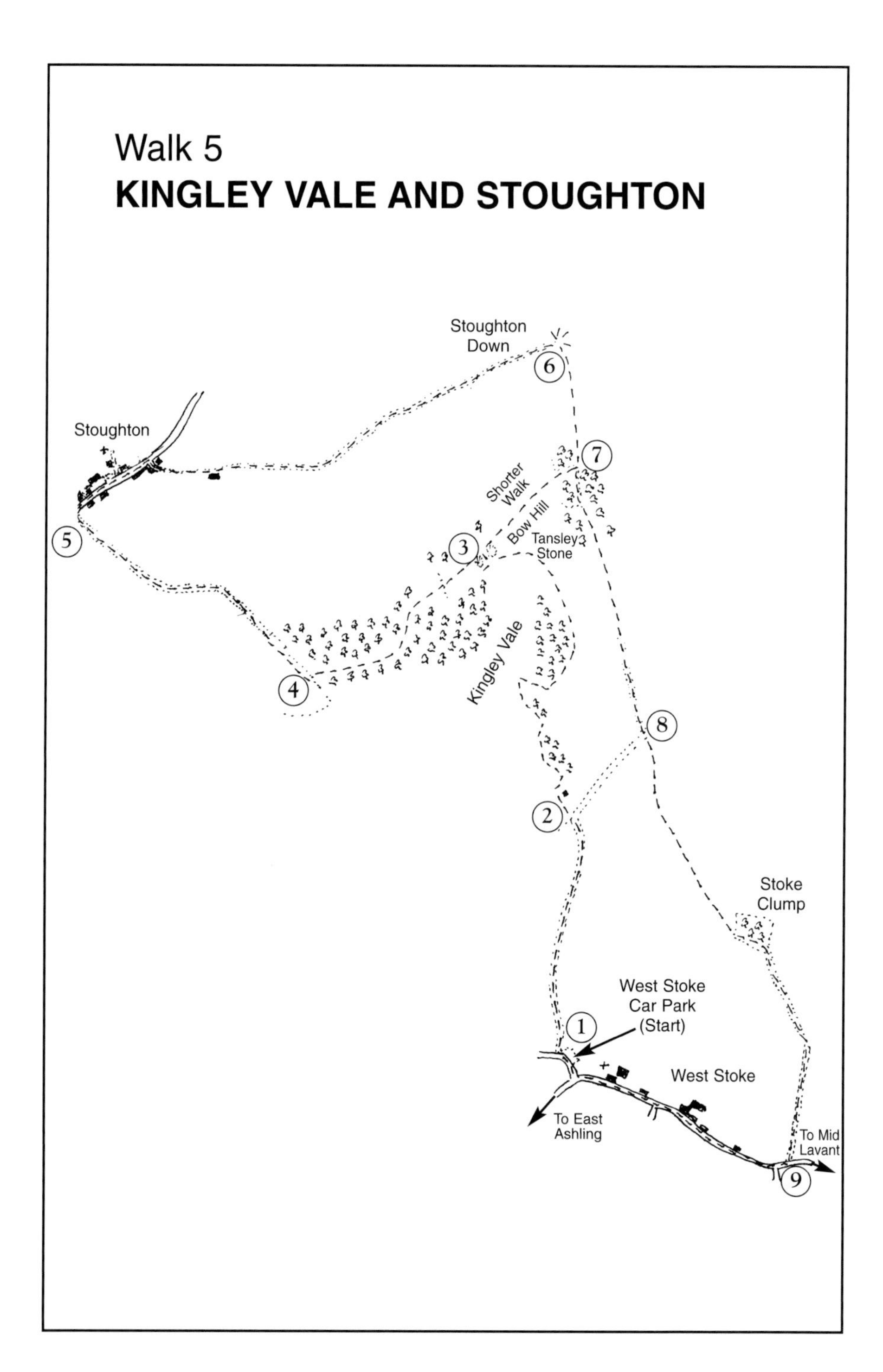
Walk 5
KINGLEY VALE AND STOUGHTON
Stoughton Down
Stoughton
Shorter Walk
Bow Hill
Tansley Stone
Kingley Vale
Stoke Clump
West Stoke Car Park (Start)
West Stoke
To East Ashling
To Mid Lavant
1
2
3
4
5
6
7
8
9

Walk 5
# KINGLEY VALE AND STOUGHTON

| | |
|---|---|
| **Distance:** | 5 or 8 miles. |
| **Route (full walk):** | West Stoke Car Park – Kingley Vale – Bow Hill – Stoughton – Stoughton Down – Bow Hill – Stoke Clump – West Stoke. |
| **Map:** | OS Explorer 120 – Chichester. |
| **Start/Parking:** | at the West Stoke Car Park, about a quarter of a mile west of the hamlet of West Stoke. Access is along an unclassified road, either from the B2178 Chichester-to-Funtington road at East Ashling or from the A286 Chichester-to-Midhurst road at Mid Lavant. The car park is about 100 yards north of a road junction at GR 824088. |
| **Public Transport:** | none. |
| **Conditions:** | the whole walk uses good well trodden paths or clear chalk and flint tracks. Half a mile of road at the end of the longer walk. |
| **Refreshments:** | Hare and Hounds pub at Stoughton (longer walk only). |

This walk earns its 'classic' status by virtue of its exploration of one of the most remarkable features in the Sussex landscape, the yew grove of Kingley Vale, which lays claim to be the finest yew forest in Europe.

The area is managed as a National Nature Reserve and as well as the 30,000 yew trees, supports 12 species of orchid, 57 varieties of breeding bird and 33 different butterfly species. You may also see Fallow Deer.

The shorter walk follows part of a numbered nature trail and encompasses the best of the reserve. The longer walk offers, in addition, an extended loop down into the next valley, visiting the downland village of Stoughton, where you will find a conveniently placed pub. Towards the end of both walks you can take another short cut from point 8 directly back to point 2.

# THE WALK

*From the far end of the car park* **(1)** *follow a gravel track for a little over half a mile to the foot of Kingley Vale. Go ahead over a stile* **(2)** *and along a track leaving a building housing a small museum on your right and also a dispenser where you should be able to collect a leaflet describing the nature trail. From here you will be following this numbered nature trail up to the top of the hill, well signed throughout. It starts by meandering between some of the oldest yew trees, gnarled and twisted like an illustration from some slightly sinister fairy tale.*

*Beyond point 11, the trail doubles back to the right and then climbs gently up the right side of the wooded combe of Kingley Vale to the summit.*

Towards the top a superb view opens out, back across Chichester Harbour to the Isle of Wight. On the right of the path is the Tansley Stone, commemorating the purchase of Kingley Vale for the nation at a time when Sir Arthur Tansley was chairman of the Nature Conservancy. On the summit you will come to two so-called bell-barrows, Bronze Age burial mounds dating from about 500 BC and known locally as 'The Devil's Humps'.

*Turn squarely right between the two bell-barrows to join a track* **(3)**. *For the shorter walk, omitting the loop down to Stoughton, turn right to follow a bridle way for about a quarter of a mile (not described in detail here). Rejoin the longer walk at point 7. For the full walk, go left along the clear track from point 3, soon re-entering woodland. At a T-junction on the edge of the wood* **(4)** *turn right and follow another good track for almost a mile down to Stoughton. Towards the bottom of the hill you will pass, on the right, a simple memorial plaque to commemorate a polish pilot officer, killed when his Hurricane aircraft crashed nearby in 1940. At the road* **(5)** *turn right and walk through the village.*

Stoughton church, hidden away to the left of the road, is well worth the small detour. Dating from the 11th century it has, unusually, remained largely unaltered.

*Continue past the Hare and Hounds pub on your left and, after another 200 yards or so, fork right along a concrete farm track. Follow this track and, subsequently, a fenced path, which climbs very gently for over a mile up on to Stoughton Down.*

*Where the path levels out at a meeting of six ways* **(6)**, *turn squarely right with a beech wood on your left. After 150 yards, fork left along a narrower path. After another 600 yards* **(7)**, *a signed bridleway coming in from your right is the end of the link route from point 3. The path continues over the scrub-covered summit of Bow Hill. Go straight over a crossing path by a nature reserve notice and begin to drop down.*

A view soon opens out across the coastal plain with the spire of Chichester Cathedral directly ahead. Away to your left is St Roche's Hill, crowned by an Iron Age fort known as The Trundle as well as prominent radio masts over the proliferation of which conservationists have fought prolonged battles in recent years.

*A track to the right* **(8)** *provides a direct route back to point 2, but the full walk continues ahead, up and over the next hill where it skirts to the right of Stoke Clump.*

*Bell Barrows, Kingley Vale.*

*View across coastal plain from Bow Hill.*

*Continue down to a road* **(9)** *where you should turn right. Follow the road for a little over half a mile, through the tiny settlement of West Stoke and back to the start.*

Walk 6

# HARTING DOWNS, BEACON HILL AND HOOKSWAY

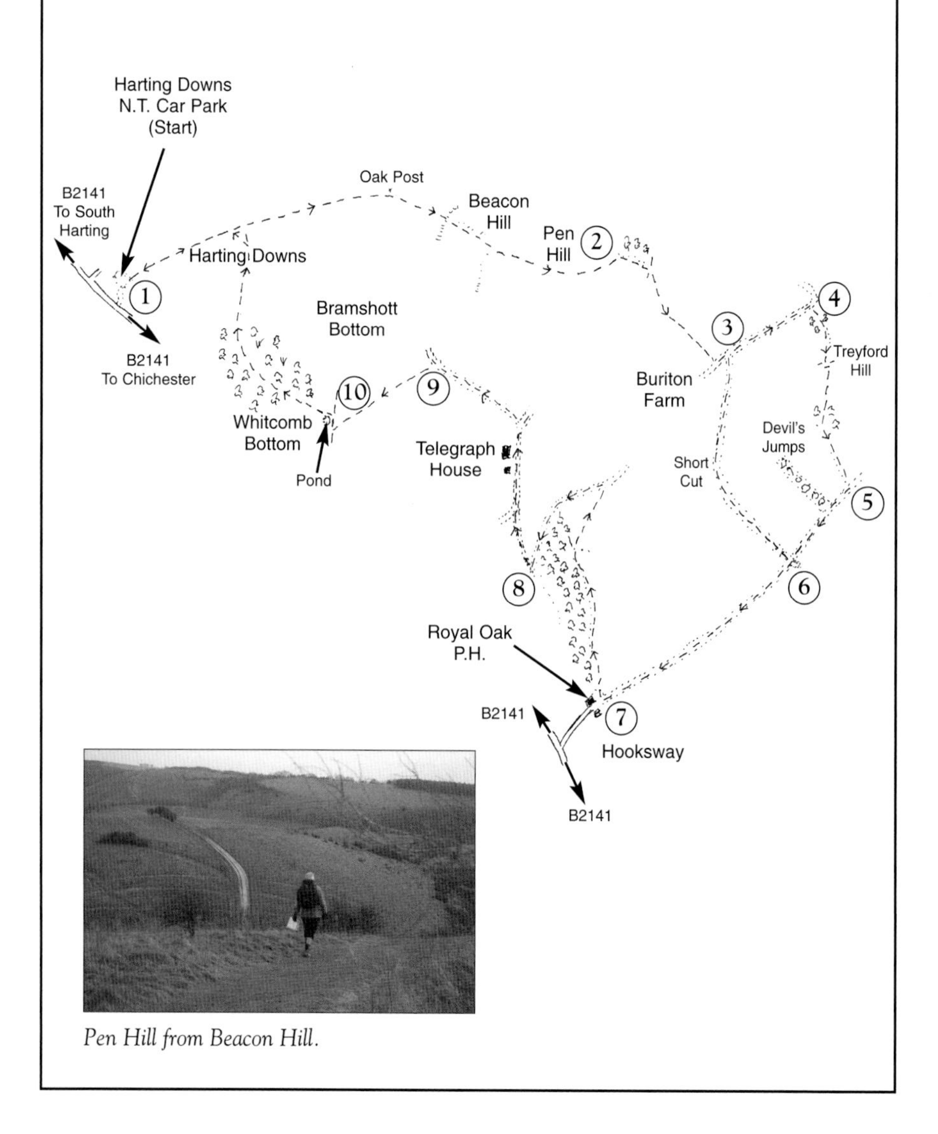


*Pen Hill from Beacon Hill.*

## Walk 6

# HARTING DOWNS, BEACON HILL AND HOOKSWAY

| | |
|---|---|
| **Distance:** | $7\frac{1}{2}$ miles. |
| **Route:** | Harting Downs Car Park – Beacon Hill – Pen Hill – Treyford Hill – Devil's Jumps – Hooksway – Telegraph House – Bramshott Bottom – Whitcomb Bottom – Harting Downs. |
| **Map:** | OS Explorer 120 – Chichester. |
| **Start/Parking:** | in the National Trust Harting Downs car park, signposted to the east of the B2141 Chichester-to-South Harting road on the summit of the Downs about a mile south of South Harting (GR 790180). |
| **Public Transport:** | none convenient. |
| **Conditions:** | fairly strenuous walking along a switchback section of the northern downs escarpment and across undulating hills and valleys to the south. All on good paths or chalk and flint tracks. |
| **Refreshments:** | Royal Oak pub at Hooksway. |

The highlight of this walk is one of the finest sections of the South Downs Way extending eastwards for over two miles across Harting Downs and on over Beacon Hill with its Iron Age hill-fort and the lower summit of Pen Hill. As a bonus I have added a short extra loop over the much less well known summit of Treyford Hill. After a pause for refreshment at Hooksway, the return route visits one of my favourite places at the southern end of the secret valley of Bramshott Bottom. Just far enough away from the 'honey-pot' of Harting Downs to retain its peaceful seclusion, this is a wonderful spot. A steady climb up the wooded side valley of Whitcomb Bottom completes a truly 'classic' circuit.

# THE WALK

*From the car park* **(1)** *start the walk eastwards along the South Downs Way which follows the top of the northern downs escarpment. After three-quarters of a mile, the path drops steeply down into a dip where there is a substantial oak waypost embedded in a flint base. From here a path climbs steeply up on to the top of Beacon Hill.*

On the 795 ft summit, next to the trig point, is a useful direction indicator. The view is immense, embracing Butser Hill and the hangers near Selbourne to the west, the extensive greensand hills to the north across the Rother valley, Leith Hill and the North Downs to the north east and the long line of the South Downs escarpment to the east. On a very clear day you can see as far as Ditchling Beacon, over 30 miles away. Looking southwards, the Isle of Wight is normally in clear view.

*After a sharp descent into another dip, go ahead over the lesser summit of Pen Hill and down the other side. At a junction* **(2)** *turn right along a wood edge, signed as the South Downs Way. Ignoring a crossing path, continue with the South Downs Way as it contours along the hill side with open fields to your right and a wooded slope dropping away to your left. Ignoring a bridleway to your left, continue across open ground where the path is unnecessarily and unpleasantly squeezed between fences.*

*At a T-junction with a substantial track turn left. After 30 yards* **(3)** *the South Downs Way goes off to the right and provides a short cut directly to point 6. This will allow you to avoid the steep ascent of Treyford Hill but also means you will miss one of the best bits of the walk. For the full circuit go ahead from point 3 on a track which soon acquires a metalled surface and begins to drop obliquely down the escarpment with a good view of the village of Treyford at the foot of the Downs. After a quarter of a mile or so* **(4)** *turn right up steps and climb steeply through woodland. Cross a track using two stiles and then follow a path left, right and up over the shoulder of Treyford Hill.*

If you are getting breathless, the view back across the Weald provides a good excuse for a rest with the promontory of Blackdown (Walk 14) clearly recognisable to the north east.

*A path winds up through an area of neglected woodland before levelling out to follow the right edge of rough pasture. Join the South Downs Way again over a stile* **(5)** *and turn right, now on a clear track.*

After 100 yards or so, a narrow path on the right provides access to the Devil's Jumps, a line of five striking Bronze Age burial mounds. Cleared from dense scrub some years ago they are now kept clear under the management of the Murray Downland Trust, named after Dr Elizabeth Murray, one of the founders of the trust and an indefatigable downland conservationist. A useful notice includes details of the site as well as an artist's impression of how the barrows might have looked in about 1500 BC.

*At a meeting of four ways* **(6)***, the South Downs Way goes off to the right, but you should go ahead (users of the short cut rejoin the walk here from the right). A clear track now descends gently for two thirds of a mile to reach the Royal Oak at Hooksway.*

This delightful isolated hostelry enjoys a perfect setting, tucked down in this quiet downland valley. The building is 400 years old and has been a pub for more than 200 of them. Between 1907 and 1971 the landlord was Alf Ainger who firmly resisted modernisation. The present landlords have extended the pub but have retained some of its original features including the brick floor and open fireplaces in the bar.

*Just short of the pub* **(7)** *turn right through the pub car park and follow a clear track along the valley. At the time of writing you have a choice of two parallel tracks. Keep to the one on the left which runs along at the foot of a wooded slope, rising up to the left. Beyond a gate, go forward along the valley floor to another gate, in sight, where you can join a track and turn sharply back to the left. Follow this fenced track up and out of the valley.*

*At the top of the hill, at a junction of tracks, turn equally sharply back to the right* **(8)**. *Shortly join and go forward along a tree-lined tarmac drive. After about half a mile, soon after passing the substantial Telegraph House on the left, fork left at a Y-junction, now back on the signposted South Downs Way. At a waypost* **(9)** *turn squarely left, leaving the South Downs Way to drop down on a wide grassy path through gorse and scrub, into the southern end of Bramshott Bottom, a delectable spot.*

*At the bottom of the hill, at another waypost, turn right along the floor of the valley, passing a small pond enclosed with a post and rail fence on your left. Immediately past the pond* **(10)**, *where the main signed path goes ahead up the combe, you should fork left along a clear path which takes you gently up along the floor of a well wooded side valley, Whitcomb Bottom. Towards the head of the valley, several paths go off to the left. Any of them will do, taking you up to rejoin the South Downs Way along the escarpment. Turn left and retrace your steps along the ridge back to the start, less than a quarter of a mile away.*

*Bramshott Bottom - Point 10.*

Walk 7

# CHILGROVE AND THE MARDENS

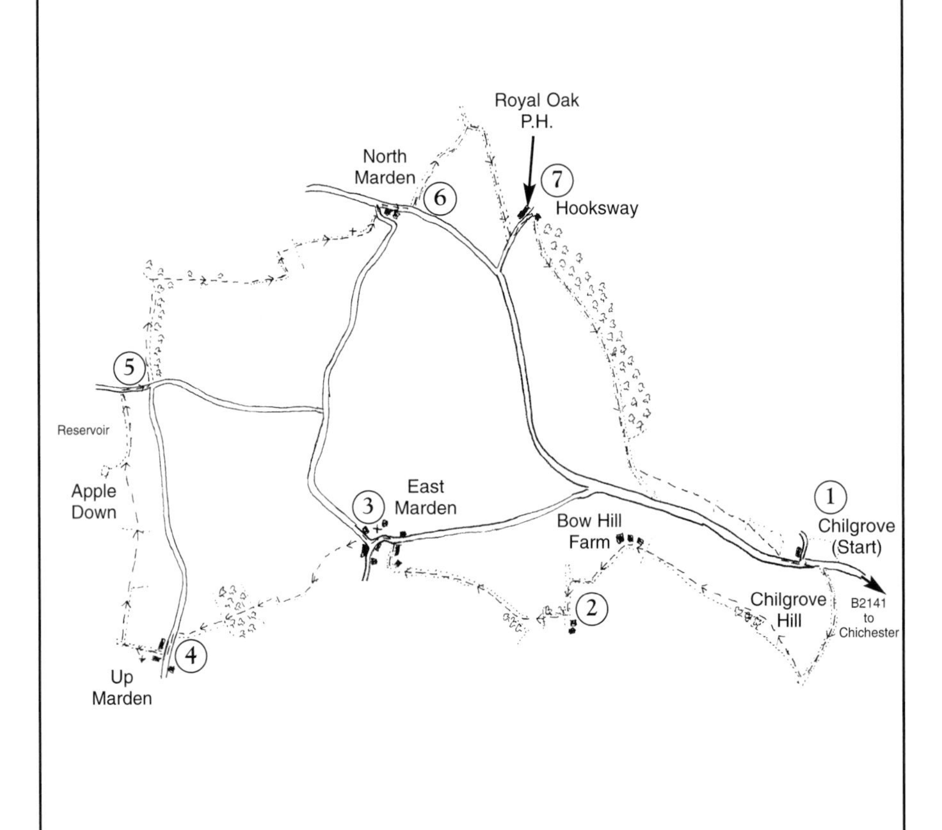

Walk 7
# CHILGROVE AND THE MARDENS

| | |
|---|---|
| **Distance:** | $7^1/_2$ miles. |
| **Route:** | Chilgrove – East Marden – Up Marden – Apple Down – North Marden – Hooksway – Chilgrove. |
| **Map:** | OS Explorer 120 – Chichester. |
| **Start/Parking:** | at Chilgrove on the B2141 Chichester-to-Harting road. There is space to park on the Green in front of the White Horse pub (GR 828144). Be sure to park in the roped-off area provided, avoiding the space reserved for pub patrons. |
| **Public Transport:** | none convenient. |
| **Conditions:** | a fairly strenuous walk across rolling downland with several ups and downs, none severe except the short sharp ascent up through woodland to Up Marden and the steep descent to East Marden, both of which may be slippery after rain. |
| **Refreshments:** | Royal Oak pub at Hooksway and the White Horse at Chilgrove. |

The southern dip slope of the Downs to the north of Chichester is a superb and surprisingly extensive stretch of gently rolling hills and quiet valleys. Lack of water has ensured that the area has never been heavily populated. The three small communities at East Marden, Up Marden, and North Marden, visited on this walk, are little more than tiny hamlets without pub or shop, but managing to sustain three downland churches, each with its own special character. Towards the end of the walk you will come across the Royal Oak pub at Hooksway, tucked down in a perfect situation at the bottom of a secluded downland valley. The White Horse Inn at the start and finish of the walk is a rather more up-market establishment, perhaps less suitable for the average walker.

The walk can easily be linked with Walk 6, the link point being at Hooksway.

# THE WALK

*From the green at Chilgrove **(1)** cross the B2141 road and start the walk along a signed bridleway, opposite. A roughly metalled track climbs steadily up on to Chilgrove Hill. At the top, turn right through a bridle gate and go forward along a grassy ridge, walking parallel to the fence on your left.*

Across this fence there is a fine view down the valley towards Stoughton (Walk 5) and Walderton with a glimpse of the coastal plain around Emsworth in the far distance. To the northwest you can pick out the distinctive shapes of Pen Hill and Beacon Hill on the Downs escarpment, rising to the heights of Harting Down (Walk 6)

*Skirt to the right of a tree clump on the summit of Chilgrove Hill and continue along the ridge, keeping to the left edge of three fields to reach Bow Hill farm. Go forward on a concrete drive past a bungalow and, very shortly, fork left over a stile, signed as a 'Footpath to East Marden'. The path skirts to the left of farm buildings and several enclosures to join a rutted track over a stile and turn right.*

*Distant view of Beacon Hill and Pen Hill from Chilgrove Hill.*

*Shortly, at another junction, go left along a metalled drive. After about 150 yards, just short of a bungalow* **(2)**, *turn right on a narrow path along the left edge of a copse to a stile. Now head straight out across a field soon dropping steeply down with East Marden in view directly ahead. Go over a stile in the bottom field corner from which a path winds through scrub, then along a right field edge and on between fences. Follow a track past the buildings at East Marden Farm, go right with the track and follow it out to a lane. Turn left past East Marden church.*

The 12th century flint church stands on raised ground overlooking the small village green and the carefully preserved thatched well house. The well provided the village water supply until as recently as 1924.

*At the road junction by the well head* **(3)**, *fork right, signposted to North Marden, Harting and Compton. After a few yards, go left over a stile and follow the direction of a sign across a meadow to a second stile and on with a fence, left. In the field corner turn right and, after 60 yards, go left over a stile. Go forward along a left field edge to a second stile beyond which a path climbs steeply up through a wood. Ignore a signed crossing path. At the top, go ahead with a hedge on your left to join a lane at Up Marden. Turn left and,*

*East Marden Church and Thatched Well Farm.*

*Up Marden Church interior.*

*just past the elaborately converted Up Marden Barn on the right* **(4)**, *turn right along the access track to Up Marden Church.*

The church, accessible along a path to the left, is a simple structure with whitewashed walls and a brick floor, still lit by candles and evoking a very special atmosphere of times past.

*Carry on along the track past the start of the church path until, after 100 yards or so, you can turn right along a right field edge. Where the fence on your right turns away to your right, go ahead without changing direction gently up across a large cultivated field on to the flat summit of Apple Down. In the next field, keep a fence on your left, eventually dropping down to join a lane. Turn right and, after about 200 yards* **(5)** *go left over a stile.*

*Follow a right field edge until, after about 500 yards you can cross a stile and bear right on a track which winds through scrub and begins to drop down within a wooded strip. Continue along a right field edge with North Marden church in view ahead. In the valley the path goes left and right, skirting to the left of a young plantation and then climbs along a left field edge to reach North Marden.*

The small church is a delight, consisting of a single room with a rounded wall at the eastern end. It has remained largely unrestored since its 12th century origins.

*Follow the access drive from the church out to the B2141 and turn right. After 100 yards* **(6)** *turn left along a tree-lined path. At a Y-junction, fork right along a more substantial track and at a lane turn left and walk down into Hooksway* **(7)**. *Opposite the Royal Oak pub, turn sharply back to the right along a dirt track, leaving the white walled Hooksway House on your left.*

*After about two thirds of a mile, about 100 yards after passing under power lines, fork left over a stile and go ahead along a low lying meadow, following a fence on your left. Go over a drive using two stiles and cross the next field to a third stile, in sight. Continue through another field, gradually converging on, and finally joining the B2141 on your right. Turn left along the grass road verge for the short distance back to the start.*

North Marden Church

# Walk 8

# BIGNOR POST, BARLAVINGTON AND SUTTON

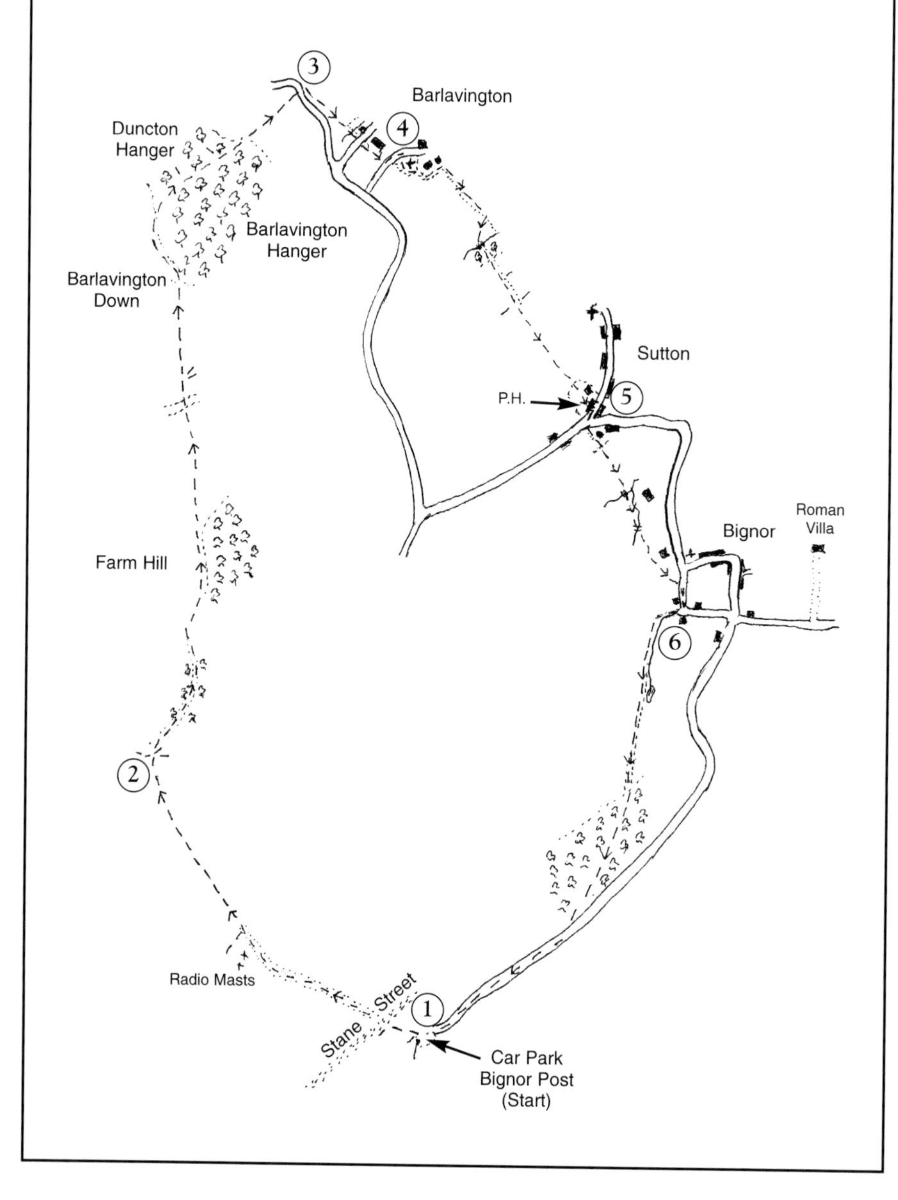

# Walk 8
# BIGNOR POST, BARLAVINGTON AND SUTTON

| | |
|---|---|
| **Distance:** | 5½ miles. |
| **Route:** | Bignor Post – Barlavington Down – Barlavington – Sutton – Bignor – Bignor Post. |
| **Map:** | OS Explorer 121 – Arundel and Pulborough. |
| **Start/Parking:** | the easiest road access is from the A29 at Bury. Follow signs through West Burton to Bignor. Just past the access to Bignor Roman Villa on your right, turn left along an unsigned lane which climbs to the top of the Downs at Bignor Post where there is a National Trust parking area (GR 974129). |
| **Public Transport:** | none. |
| **Conditions:** | a fairly hilly walk, much of it along good paths or chalk and flint tracks. The path between Sutton and Bignor is likely to be very muddy in places. |
| **Refreshments:** | White Horse pub at Sutton. |

The highlight of this exceptional walk is the superb stretch of bridleway from the start at Bignor Post. Surprisingly the planners of the South Downs Way ignored this prime route along the top of the wooded downland escarpment to Barlavington Down in favour of a considerably less attractive bridleway through Littleton Farm to the south.

A fine descent through Duncton Hanger brings us to the tiny hamlet of Barlavington. From here a series of footpaths traverse low, gently undulating downland foothills, crossing three tiny streams which arise from the 'spring line' at the foot of the chalk to flow northwards into the Weald to join the River Rother, a tributary of the Arun. Sutton is a more substantial village with a welcoming pub, conveniently situated about two thirds of the way round the walk.

From the edge of the village of Bignor the walk can be extended by a mile or so to explore the village and to visit the nearby Roman Villa. A final well graded climb takes us up through more woodland and back to the start.

# THE WALK

*The walk starts from the carved oak Bignor Post* **(1)** *next to the car parking area. Set out along a track, not signed on the post, which starts to the right of a 'No Cars' notice. Follow this clear flint track, ignoring side and crossing paths, including the South Downs Way where it soon goes off to the left.*

The track crosses the line of Stane Street, worthy of a 'there and back' detour if time permits. This Roman Road once linked London with Chichester. The raised bank or agger on which the road ran, was originally constructed using rammed flint and chalk, topped with flint and gravel and is easily recognisable in places, as are traces of the flanking draining ditches.

*The track climbs very gradually with a wide view opening up to the north across the Weald. On the right is a nicely preserved dew pond. The track passes about 150 yards to the right of the twin radio masts and then begins to drop down where you should ignore a signed bridleway to the left. After leaving the National Trust area the path descends, unfenced, across open cultivated downland. About 40 yards short of a gate* **(2)** *fork right along a narrow path. After a few yards, at a T-junction, bear right and, after a few more yards, where you have a choice of three paths ahead, take the one on the left.*

*A tree lined path follows a fairly level course across a wide flat dip in the escarpment and on round the right shoulder of Farm Hill before opening out across another shallow dip. Keep with the main track, ignoring a crossing track and two side paths to the right, soon climbing fairly steeply up on to Barlavington Down.*

Towards the top a well placed seat provides a good spot for a rest and a look back along the line of the Downs escarpment. On a clear day you should be able to see as far

*The path on Farm Hill.*

as the promontory of Wolstonbury Hill, with the intermediate landmarks of Chanctonbury Ring and the masts on Truleigh Hill easily identifiable. A young beech plantation on the hillside in front of you will eventually obscure this exceptional view.

*Continue along the upper edge of woodland, dropping away to your right. Enter the wood and descend. At a path junction in front of a large beech tree, fork right and follow this clear path down through the wood and on between fences to join a lane. Go over the stile opposite* **(3)** *and bear right across a field, following the direction of a footpath sign. Depending on the season there is usually a faint trodden path. Go over a second stile, join a hedge, left, and follow it down to a stile in the field corner. A clear path now crosses a lane and a stream in a dip and climbs, passing a massive ancient yew tree. Continue out via an access drive to join a lane at Barlavington and turn left. After 100 yards or so* **(4)** *go right through a gate into Barlavington churchyard.*

The church is a simple 13th century structure with a plain interior and a small bell tower. In the churchyard is an improvised seat, carved out of a tree trunk, from which there is a good view southwards towards the tree covered downland escarpment.

*Walk round behind the church, leave the churchyard through another gate and go forward along a track, soon bearing left, leaving the buildings of Barlavington Farm on your left. Shortly, turn right along a broad grass strip until you can go right over a stile and ahead across a sloping meadow, soon bearing left to cross a stream and climb through a small wood. The path continues up along the left edge of rough pasture. At the top go directly ahead across an open cultivated field, on through a garden and out past a house to join lane at Sutton, next to the White Horse* **(5)**.

*Turn right past the pub and, immediately, at a road junction, go ahead on a narrow path between the two roads, signposted as a footpath to Bignor. After a short enclosed path go directly ahead across two fields dropping down to cross a stream. A path, muddy underfoot in places, winds through a wooded valley and climbs past a cottage to join a lane. Turn right.*

*After about 100 yards* **(6)**, *to return to Bignor Post, turn right along a track which, particularly after rain, doubles as a stream.*

If you have time follow the 'square' of lanes around the picturesque village of Bignor and on to visit the Bignor Roman Villa (see sketch map). A farmer ploughing a field to the east of the village first discovered the villa in 1811. Subsequent excavation, started in 1827, revealed that this was once a large country house, occupied between the 2nd and 4th centuries. It contains some remarkably well preserved mosaic pavements. The Roman Villa is open to the public, March, April, May and October, 10 to 5 (closed Mondays except BH), June to September, 10 to 6 daily.

*Return to point 6 and resume the main walk along the track described above, crossing a short sleeper causeway and continuing beside the stream. After 100 yards or so, fork left over a stile and go forward along the left edge of three fields, on a headland path at first, then between fences, as the path commences its steady climb back up on to the Downs. After entering woodland, turn right at a T-junction with a track. After a few yards, fork left along a narrower path, which climbs obliquely up the wooded slope, eventually joining the road up to Bignor Post which you can now follow back up to the top of the hill and the car park.*

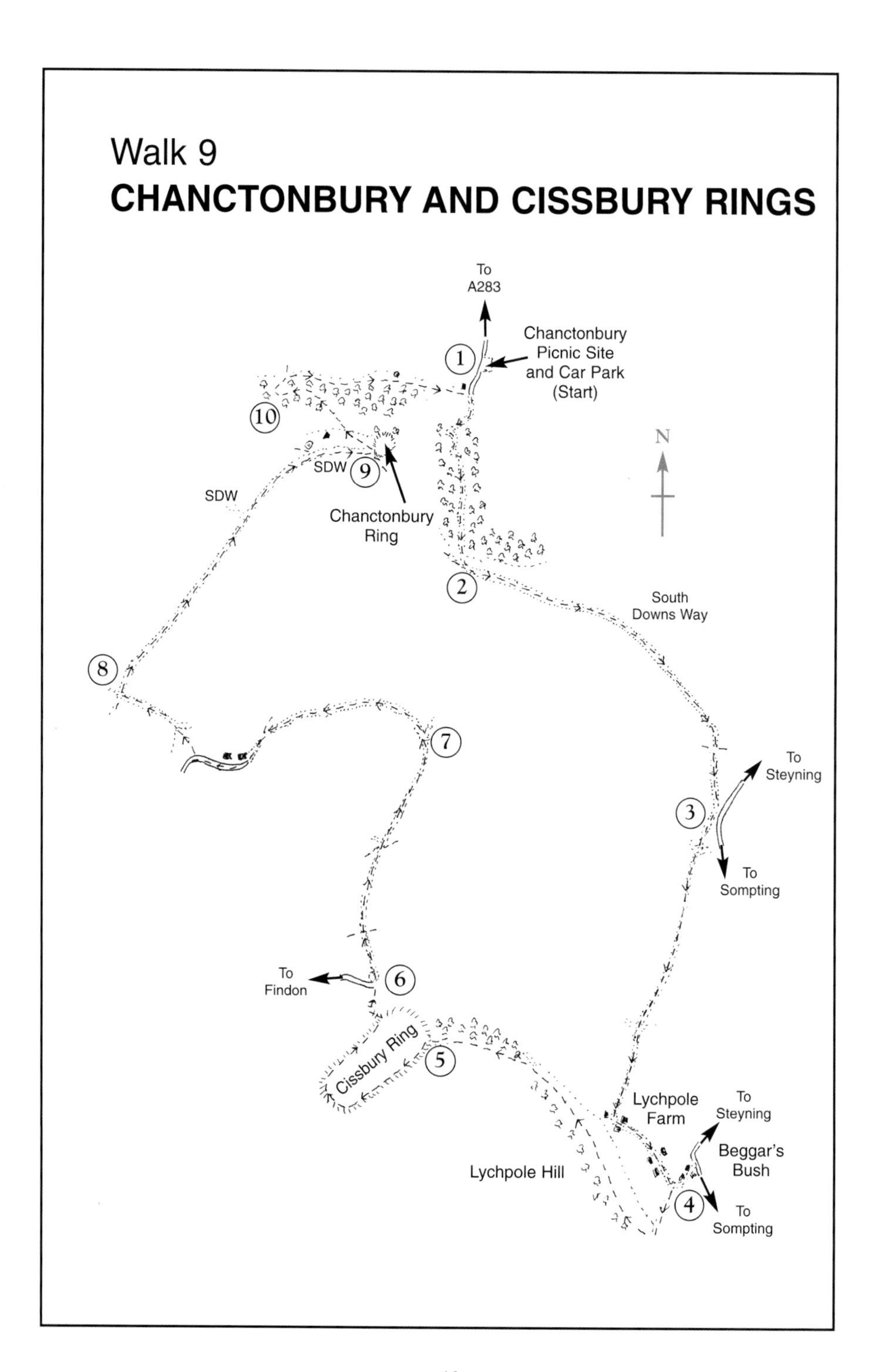
Walk 9
CHANCTONBURY AND CISSBURY RINGS
To
A283
Chanctonbury
Picnic Site
and Car Park
(Start)
1
10
N
SDW
9
SDW
Chanctonbury
Ring
2
South
Downs Way
8
7
To
Steyning
3
To
Sompting
To
Findon
6
Cissbury Ring
5
Lychpole
Farm
To
Steyning
Beggar's
Bush
Lychpole Hill
4
To
Sompting

## Walk 9
# CHANCTONBURY AND CISSBURY RINGS

| | |
|---|---|
| **Distance:** | 12 miles. |
| **Route:** | Chanctonbury picnic site – Wiston Bostal –South Downs Way – Top of Steyning Bowl – Lychpole Farm – Beggar's Bush – Cissbury Ring – Findon Park – Chanctonbury Ring – Chanctonbury picnic site. |
| **Map:** | OS Explorer 121: Arundel and Pulborough. |
| **Start/Parking:** | at the Chanctonbury car park and picnic site at the foot of the northern Downs escarpment. Follow a lane, signposted to Chanctonbury Ring, southwards from the A283 Steyning-to-Pulborough road about a mile east of Washington. The car park is at GR 146125. |
| **Public Transport:** | none convenient. |
| **Conditions:** | mostly on firm chalk and flint tracks. One sharp climb at the start, then across rolling downland with several more ups and downs, none severe. |
| **Refreshments:** | none on the route. |

This walk explores an extensive area of open rolling downland to the north of Worthing. Starting at the foot of the northern downland escarpment we climb steadily to the summit of the Downs using one of the many well graded downland 'bostal' paths which have, for hundreds of years, provided access to the high ground and which are such a characteristic feature of the northern scarp slope. We can then stride out across high open rolling hills. Although this is the longest walk in this collection, the 'going' is invariably good and you will not have to contend with a single stile on the entire 12-mile circuit. The highlights of the walk are provided by the twin 'rings' of Cissbury and Chanctonbury, both hilltops crowned with Iron Age forts. Until it was struck down in the Great Gale of 1987, the curved windswept silhouette of the clump of trees on Chanctonbury had become something of a symbol of the South Downs. It has now been partially replanted and will surely one day be restored to its former glory.

# THE WALK

*From the car park entrance* **(1)** *turn left along the lane and head for the Downs, ignoring signed paths to right and left. The lane dwindles to a track and climbs steadily up to the summit of the escarpment. Keep to the main well graded track, ignoring various unofficial side paths. At the top of the hill* **(2)***, at a junction of tracks, turn left, now on the South Downs Way which you will be following for almost two miles.*

As you proceed, a succession of views unfold. Firstly to the north across a wide Wealden panorama, then southwards across lower hills to the heights of Cissbury Ring. Then, away to your left, a series of receding whale back promontories along the downland escarpment to the east, – furthest away the outliers of Wolstonbury and Newtimber Hills and, nearer, Truleigh Hill with its prominent radio masts. Finally, ahead, you get a glimpse of Brighton and the sea.

*Follow the South Downs Way until you reach a point just short of where it reaches the Steyning Bostal road* **(3)***. Don't join the road. Instead, go ahead along a roughly metalled track which diverges from the road, across level ground at first. Go straight across a concrete farm track and shortly descend into Lychpole Bottom. Ignore a second crossing track. Follow the main track as it bears left past the buildings at Lychpole Farm and continues as a concrete farm access drive, passing some ugly modern barns.*

*Where the concrete drive turns squarely left at Beggar's Bush* **(4)***, you should turn right, leaving two more barns on your right, to follow a wide fenced track. After about 300 yards, fork right along a grassy path and, after another 30 yards, go through a bridle gate where there is a rather misleading waymark. Bear right along a faint path which contours along the lower slope of Lychpole Hill with a scrub covered hillside rising up to your left. The path is all the better for being open and unfenced.*

*After almost a mile, go through two bridle gates and fork left, uphill, leaving a National Trust notice 'Cissbury Ring' on your right. Towards the top of the hill* **(5)** *with the ramparts of Cissbury Ring immediately ahead, go half left through two gates and up to a gap in the ring where you can turn left up steps on to the top of the grass covered ramparts. Follow the top of the main inner ring of Cissbury clockwise for the best part of a mile.*

Cissbury Ring, named after the Saxon conqueror Cissa, is one of the largest and most spectacular prehistoric sites on the South Downs, comprising a double rampart and ditch dating from the Iron Age. The whole area stands at over 600 feet above sea level with spectacular views in all directions. The area, in the hands of the National Trust, is managed to conserve wild life, including several varieties of orchid and 28 species of butterfly including the rare Adonis Blue.

*When you are about three quarters of the way round the circuit of Cissbury, double back to the left down steps through scrub to reach a small car park at the end of a narrow road coming up from Findon to the west* **(6)***. Go straight ahead along a fenced track,* *leaving the small parking area on your left. Ignore a crossing path and go ahead with the patchy remains of Chanctonbury Ring more or less directly ahead.*

*At a complex junction of tracks go ahead, ignoring a right fork and two tracks off to the left. After about 650 yards, soon after passing a small wood on your right* **(7)** *fork left on a track, level at first, then dropping down into a valley. Towards the bottom, ignore a signed path doubling back to the right and after a few yards, where you have a choice of parallel track and road ahead, follow the road on the left which soon heads generally westwards along the valley.*

*After about a quarter of a mile fork right through an iron gate, drop diagonally down across a paddock to a bridle gate and go forward along a hard track. The track climbs at first then drops down to cross a dip with a good view of Chanctonbury Ring up the valley to the right. Climb again and, where the ground levels out* **(8)** *turn right along a wide crossing track and follow it for one and a half miles up to Chanctonbury Ring.*

Towards the top the track passes through an open area of grassland which has been designated under the Countryside Stewardship Scheme, protecting the downland turf and allowing open public access at least until September 2112. This permits you to divert left up to the trig point on Chanctonbury Hill, a magnificent view point. To the north, on a clear day you can see as far as Leith Hill and the North Downs. The foreground is only slightly marred by unsightly sandpits at the foot of the Downs and the rapidly expanding village of Ashington, the site of rampant new house building. Also on the left of the path is a dewpond, restored by the Society of Sussex Downsmen in 1970.

*Just short of Chanctonbury Ring* **(9)**, *double back to the left dropping down to a bridle gate from which a terraced path continues obliquely down the partly wooded northern escarpment. At the bottom of the hill at a T-junction* **(10)**, *turn right walking within the bottom edge of the wooded slope. Where you have a choice of three waymarked paths, keep right, still within the lower edge of the wood.*

*Chanctonbury Ring from track between points 8 and 9.*

*After two thirds of a mile you will come to a junction with your outgoing route where you can turn left for a few yards back to start.*

Walk 10

# DEVIL'S DYKE, NEWTIMBER HILL AND POYNINGS

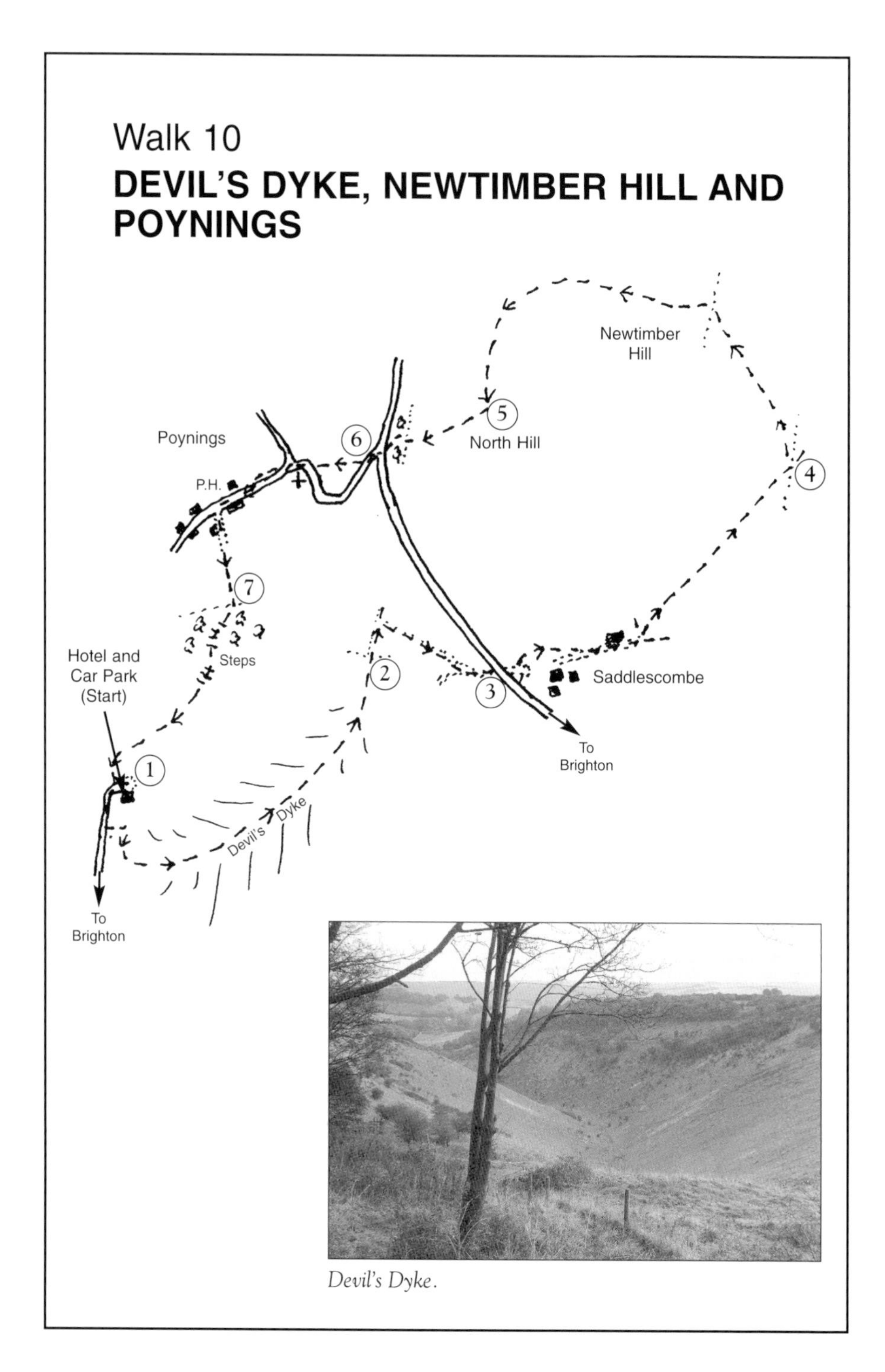


*Devil's Dyke.*

# Walk 10
## DEVIL'S DYKE, NEWTIMBER HILL AND POYNINGS

| | |
|---|---|
| **Distance:** | 4 miles. |
| **Route:** | Devil's Dyke Hotel – Devil's Dyke – Saddlescombe – Newtimber Hill – Poynings – Devil's Dyke Hotel. |
| **Map:** | OS Explorer 122: South Downs Way – Steyning to Newhaven. |
| **Start/Parking:** | in the car park next to the Devil's Dyke Hotel (GR 258110). The easiest access is from the Brighton bypass at the Dyke Road interchange. |
| **Public Transport:** | special limited summer bus service from Brighton. |
| **Conditions:** | mostly on good paths or across open grass downland. Two steep climbs and one sharp descent across grass. |
| **Refreshments:** | pubs at Devil's Dyke, next to the start and at Poynings. |

Although this is one of the shorter walks in this book, it is also one of the most strenuous. You will have to tackle two significant climbs, the generally well graded ascent to the summit of Newtimber Hill from Saddlescombe and a final steep ascent from Poynings back up on to the top of the Downs escarpment, 700 ft above sea level, where the walk starts and finishes.

Much of the walk crosses land managed by the National Trust who have recently taken over the care of the Devil's Dyke and the surrounding area and extended their holding on Newtimber Hill. The Dyke is still a major tourist 'honeypot' but the Trust should be able to fend off the sort of commercial developments which have disfigured the area in the past, including, at different times, a zoo and fairground. Accessible now only by car, a seasonal bus service or on foot, it was, until 1938, served by rail from Brighton. At the turn of the last century a funicular railway, the scars of which can be seen towards the end of the walk, took passengers up the northern escarpment from Poynings.

The main feature of the walk is the Devil's Dyke itself, seen at its most dramatic as we traverse the whole length of this deep and narrow natural combe, taking us quickly away from the crowds around the hotel area.

# THE WALK

*From the car park* **(1)** *walk back along the access road. After about 100 yards, turn left along a signposted bridleway and after another 60 yards; turn sharply back to the right to go through a bridle gate. A path curves round to the left and drops down into and along the floor of the deep rift of the Devil's Dyke with steep grassy slopes rising up on either side.*

A quiet and unspoilt spot today, it is amazing to think that, at one time, a cable car operated from one side of the Dyke to the other.

*At the far end of the Dyke* **(2)** *where you have a choice of stile, field gate and bridle gate in front of you, go through the bridle gate on the right, joining a bridleway which has come down the hill from behind on the right. At a way post turn right up a short steep scrub-covered slope to a stile and go forward on a path along the left edge of a field with a grassy slope rising up on your right. Join and follow a metalled access drive out to the road at Saddlescombe* **(3)**.

*Follow the private road to Saddlescombe Farm opposite and, after 50 yards, go left through a bridle gate, waymarked as the South Downs Way. A path skirts to the left of farm buildings to join a farm access road.*

Saddlescombe Farm, now part of the National Trust estate and housing their local headquarters, is notable for a donkey wheel, in use until 1910 to bring water up from a well, 175 ft deep.

*Just beyond the last farm cottage on the left, go through a bridle gate and, after 20 yards, turn left through a second bridle gate. After another 20 yards fork right along an unfenced track which climbs steadily up a ridge on to Newtimber Hill. At the top* **(4)**, *just short of a bridle gate and a National Trust notice, turn squarely left across open downland, keeping to the top of the ridge.*

The view back across to Devil's Dyke and along the line of the western Downs is second to none. As you proceed another view opens out to the right towards Wolstonbury Hill and the Weald beyond.

*You are soon faced with a fence and must detour to the right to find a gate in it. Once through this gate, resume your previous direction across the flat summit of Newtimber Hill through an area of pasture and patchy scrub. The path is a bit vague but if you keep to the highest ground and head generally west you won't go wrong.*

*After about 300 yards the path is a little more distinct as it veers round to the left and heads back towards Devil's Dyke, dropping into a shallow dip with the slope of North Hill ahead. Once down into this dip* **(5)** *veer half right towards the edge of the hill. Very shortly, the village of Poynings comes into sight directly ahead, tucked down at the foot of the Downs.*

*Drop steeply down the grassy hillside, aiming for Poynings Church. There is no defined path and some care is now needed to find your way off the hill. Towards the bottom of the slope you will come to a fence and an impenetrable belt of scrub. Turn right here beside the fence to join a path which has been recently levelled and improved. Shortly, where the main path goes ahead along the side of the hill, you should fork left down steps to a stile in a fence.*

*Poynings from Newtimber Hill.*

*Beyond this stile turn left to follow a narrow path which winds through an uneven area of old quarry workings to join a road opposite a junction.*

*Follow the road opposite, and after 30 yards* **(6)**, *go right through scrub to a stile, down across pasture and out via a farm drive to the road opposite Poynings Church.*

*Turn right to a road junction, cross the road and go through a brick archway, opposite, from which a path runs parallel to the road into Poynings village. Follow the road past the Royal Oak pub on your right. After a few more yards turn left along Dyke Lane, signed as a bridleway which soon becomes a fenced path and heads for the Downs which loom up rather formidably ahead.*

*At the foot of the tree covered slope where there is a National Trust notice 'Devil's Dyke'* **(7)**, *fork right on a path which takes you up 192 steps through the wood to a path junction where you should go right through a swing gate. After another 62 steps the gradient eases as the path climbs more gently along a terrace with superb views westwards along the Downs. The prominent village in the foreground is Fulking.*

Towards the top of the hill you will cross a grassy trough which takes a straight line down the steep slope. This is all that remains of the late Victorian funicular railway.

*Very shortly go left through a swing gate. A final short climb brings you back to the start.*

Walk 11

# BERWICK, ALCISTON AND THE EAST SUSSEX DOWNS

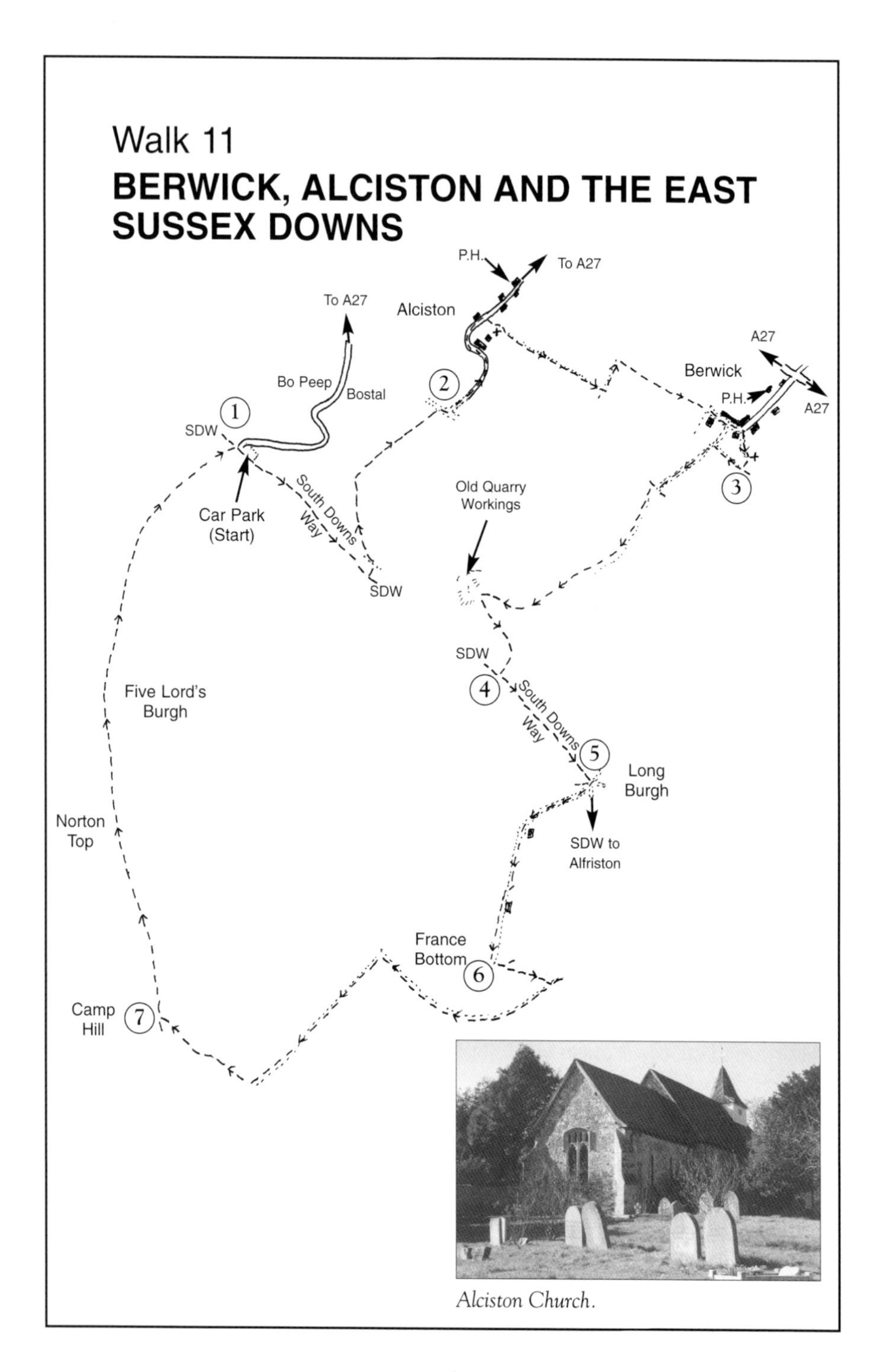


*Alciston Church.*

## Walk 11
# BERWICK, ALCISTON AND THE EAST SUSSEX DOWNS

| | |
|---|---|
| **Distance:** | 8¼ miles. |
| **Route:** | Bo-peep Bostal – South Downs Way – Alciston – Berwick – South Downs Way – Long Burgh – France Bottom – Camp Hill – Five Lord's Burgh – Bo-peep Bostal. |
| **Map:** | OS Explorer 123: South Downs Way – Newhaven to Eastbourne. |
| **Start/Parking:** | in the car park at the top of Bo-peep Bostal (GR 493050). Access is via a narrow lane which heads southwards from the A27 Lewes-to-Eastbourne road about 300 yards on the Eastbourne side of the Barley Mow pub at Selmeston. |
| **Public Transport:** | scanty weekday bus service from Lewes along the A27. Join the walk at Berwick. |
| **Conditions:** | generally easy walking, mostly on firm tracks or good paths. One steady climb up the Downs escarpment. |
| **Refreshments:** | Rose Cottage Inn at Alciston, Cricketer's Inn at Berwick, both a short distance off the described walk. |

This 8 mile circuit certainly has many of the classic ingredients of a good downland walk - two delightful villages on the spring line at the foot of the Downs, both with excellent pubs; two downland churches with contrasting ancient and modern historical associations; two of the glorious terraced bostal paths which are such a splendid and characteristic feature of the northern downs escarpment; the secret unspoilt combe of France Bottom; and above all, the opportunity to stride out for several miles across high open downland with spectacular views all the way.

# THE WALK

*From the car park* **(1)** *start the walk eastwards along the South Downs Way climbing gently over the 600 ft summit of Bostal Hill on an unfenced track with fine views southwards to Newhaven and the sea and northwards over a wide expanse of the Weald. After half a mile, at a four-armed fingerpost, turn squarely left across grass. After a few yards a stile comes into view ahead beyond which a terraced bostal path bears left dropping obliquely down the scarp slope. At the bottom of the steepest part of the slope go over a stile to enter a sunken tree-lined path which eventually emerges to follow a right field edge.*

*At a junction with a track* **(2)** *turn right and after 60 yards go left along another track which becomes a lane and takes you into the village of Alciston.*

You will pass to the left of the fine old tithe barn and to the right of the walled village pond. Then on your right across a paddock you get a good view of the remains of a medieval dovecote.

*Turn right along the path to the 13th century flint church. Just short of the steps up into the churchyard, go left through a squeeze stile and follow the churchyard wall to another stile. Go right through a gap and left along a left field edge with the spire of Berwick church directly ahead. In the field corner go forward through another gap and left along another left field edge until you can go right along an unfenced strip across a large field, aiming for Berwick once more. A farm track continues out to a lane.*

*The Cricketer's Inn is now along the lane to the left but, to continue the walk, turn right along the concrete access drive to Berwick Church, walk through the church car park and along a gravel path to the church.*

Berwick Church is notable for a number of modern mural paintings painted by Duncan Grant, Vanessa Bell and Quentin Bell, members of the so-called Bloomsbury Group, who lived at Charleston Farmhouse, nearby. They depict biblical scenes in modern settings.

*At the church entrance, follow the path round to the right, leaving the church and churchyard on your left. At a T-junction with a track* **(3)** *where a sudden view opens out southwards to the Downs, turn right. After 250 yards turn left and head for the Downs. At a third T-junction go right for 10 yards only before turning left along a hedged path and heading for the Downs once more. A path continues along the foot of a grassy bank and then zigzags right and left up to the top of the escarpment on a fine well-graded terraced path, passing an area of old chalk quarry workings.*

*At the summit go forward for 50 yards, descending gently between widely spaced fences to a junction with the South Downs Way* **(4)** *where you should turn left. Follow this unfenced chalk and flint track for half a mile across high open downland.*

Views now open up ahead across the Cuckmere valley to the Downs rising up to High and Over, seaward to Cuckmere Haven and the first of the Seven Sisters, and the village of Alfriston tucked down in the valley directly ahead.

*At a meeting of six ways* **(5)** *turn squarely right along a clear track, the only one of the six which is marked with a yellow arrow indicating footpath status. It passes between areas of thick scrub and then to the right of a house and garden. About 100 yards short of a second* *house side step to the right over a stile and resume your previous direction, now with a hedge on your left, soon dropping steeply down into France Bottom.*

The whole of the hillside to your right as well as France Bottom is presently open for public access under the Countryside Stewardship Scheme though this may not continue beyond September 2112.

*At the bottom of the hill* **(6)** *turn left over a stile and immediately fork right on a path which climbs obliquely up out of the valley.*

This area is being managed as part of the so-called Sussex Downs Environmentally Sensitive Area. At the time of writing a number of Exmoor Ponies have been imported to graze the land in an attempt to control the invasive Tor Grass and allow indigenous chalk downland flower species to flourish.

*At the top of the slope, go over a stile and double back to the right along an enclosed bridleway which continues to climb gently with a bird's eye view of France Bottom to your right. Follow the main bridleway, ignoring two more access points into the Countryside Stewardship area to your right. Just beyond the highest point turn squarely left and follow the bridleway down beside a fence into the next valley. At the bottom follow the path right and left through an area of patchy scrub to a path junction where you should turn right. A path soon climbs obliquely up the scrub-covered slope.*

*At the top* **(7)** *turn right along a wide track. Ignoring all side paths, follow this splendid grassy track for a mile and a half along an undulating ridge, crossing the low summit of Norton Top and past a place called Five Lord's Burgh, once the site of five burial mounds, though only three now remain. A gentle but steady climb takes you back to the summit of the escarpment and the start of the walk.*

*Exmoor Ponies grazing in France Bottom.*

## Walk 12
# BURPHAM AND THE ARUN VALLEY

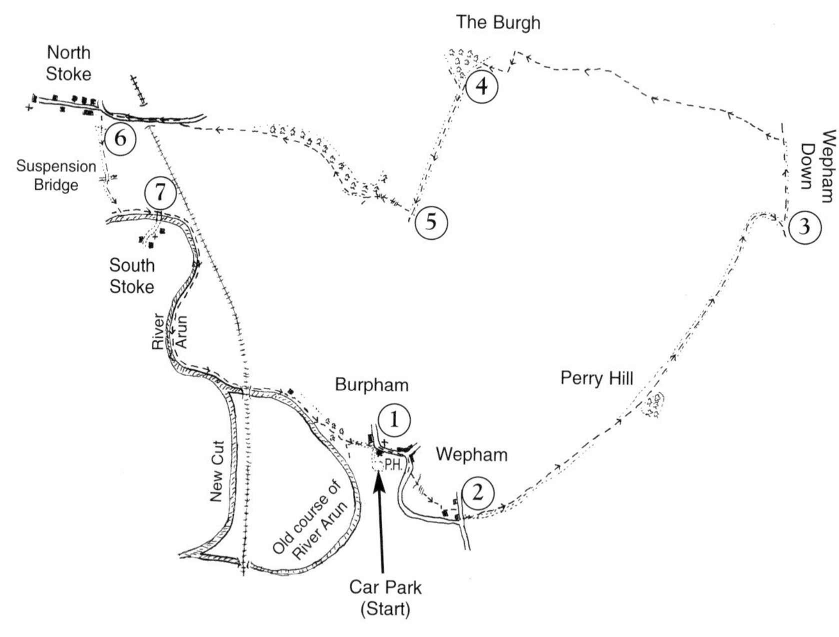

*River Arun near South Stoke-Arundel Park in background.*

Walk 12

# BURPHAM AND THE ARUN VALLEY

| | |
|---|---|
| **Distance:** | 7½ miles. |
| **Route:** | Burpham – Wepham – Perry Hill – Wepham Down –The Burgh – North Stoke – South Stoke – Burpham. |
| **Map:** | OS Explorer 121: Arundel and Pulborough. |
| **Start/Parking:** | the village of Burpham, signposted along a three-mile cul-de-sac northwards from the A27 east of Arundel Station. Park in the Burpham recreation ground car park behind the George and Dragon pub at GR 039088. |
| **Public Transport:** | none. |
| **Conditions:** | excellent walking along good downland tracks and a raised grassy river bank. One steady climb and one steep descent. The path beyond point 5 may be swampy after heavy rain. |
| **Refreshments:** | George and Dragon pub at Burpham. |

The Arun, Adur and Cuckmere rivers have created the only major gaps in the 80 mile ridge of the Sussex Downs, allowing us, within the compass of a relatively short walk, to enjoy the contrast between high open downland and tranquil river bank. This is certainly one of the best of these varied walks, starting and finishing at the hamlet of Burpham, tucked away at the end of a cul-de-sac on a low plateau on the eastern side of the Arun valley.

The walk climbs quickly out of the village to follow the fine grassy ridge of Perry Hill with glorious views across the Arun valley to Arundel Park. Good tracks cross rolling downland before a steep descent takes us down into the valley to join the river. Short and worthwhile detours allow visits to the twin hamlets of North and South Stoke, both with charming small churches.

# THE WALK

*From the car park* **(1)** *return to the lane by the George and Dragon pub and turn right. At a road junction fork right and, after less than 100 yards go left over a stile, across a low-lying meadow and a stream and up steps to a second stile. Beyond the stile where you have a choice of signed paths keep left, heading out across grass to find another stile and a narrow path which squeezes between gardens and out via an access drive to join a lane.*

*Turn right and, after 100 yards* **(2)**, *go left along a roughly metalled access drive. After a few yards, this becomes an unmade track which climbs steadily up on to the Downs. Beyond a stile the right of way officially follows a right field edge, parallel to the main track. Both track and field path are well used by walkers and rejoin towards the top of the hill, at a signed path junction, fork left along the ridge of Perry Hill. Follow a fence along the ridge for over a mile.*

The views from Perry Hill are superb, with Burpham in the foreground and, beyond, the wide Arun valley backed by the heights of Arundel Park. Downstream the valley opens out with Arundel Castle guarding the gap and the distant coastal plain beyond.

*At the highest point on the ridge path, ignore a track off to the right up to a seat next to the circular Norfolk Clump of trees. From here you will be walking along a more substantial track which finally curves round to the right, almost doubling back on itself. Just short of a wide gateway where the track acquires a concrete surface* **(3)**, *you should double sharply back to the left along a dirt track with a fence, right, across the plateau of Wepham Down.*

*After a little over a quarter of a mile, go through a gate, forward through a second gateway and fork left along a wide unfenced track which crosses a broad shallow dip where you should ignore a crossing path. At a T-junction at a place known as The Burgh turn left and, after less than 100 yards, fork right, skirting round to the left of an area of scrub. After another 200 yards or so* **(4)**, *ignore a right fork, leaving an area of woodland on your right. Ignoring a path to the right, continue with the main track which contours along the hillside as the ground drops away to your right into the Arun valley. The little hamlet of South Stoke, which you will be passing later in the walk, is now in clear view.*

*After about half a mile* **(5)**, *at a waypost, turn sharply right to follow a narrow fenced path down into the valley. It is steep and slippery in places but steps have been provided to help you down the steepest bit. At the bottom of the hill go forward through a gate (not the one on the left). A path now follows the foot of a wooded slope rising up to your right. Carry on through three more gates, and gently up across a field to join a lane and go left along it. Just short of a telephone box the walk continues over a stile on your left* **(6)**.

If time permits follow the lane ahead into the tiny hamlet of North Stoke, recorded in the Doomsday survey but now maintaining a population of less than 50. The church, a few minutes walk away, is worth a detour. Although no longer used

*South Stoke.*

for worship, it has been carefully maintained by the Churches Conservation Trust. It dates from the 12th to 14th centuries and contains a fine old font of local Pulborough stone.

*From the stile at point 6 follow a well trodden path which soon crosses a farm track and then drops down beside a fence to an unusual suspension bridge. A well maintained path follows a raised bank through a swampy area to join the River Arun. Bear left and follow the river bank downstream.*

A substantial bridge provides access to South Stoke, once again worth a detour as far as the church which, although much restored, has a slim elegant tower and a Norman south door.

*To continue the walk, don't cross the bridge* **(7)**. *Instead, carry on downstream along the raised left bank of the Arun. After a little over half a mile the waterway divides. The main channel, a 'new cut', constructed in 1860 at the time of the building of the railway, bears away to the right. Our path follows the bank of the original river, now reduced to a quiet backwater, over the railway and on along the top of a grassy bank.*

*Cross two stiles, skirting to the right of a ruined ivy-covered building, and continue beside the water with a grassy bank rising up across the meadow on your left, a lovely sheltered spot. The solid square tower of Burpham church is soon glimpsed through the trees ahead. After another 250 yards or so, a trodden path diverges from the river bank to climb obliquely up a scrub covered slope. At a junction turn left along a wider track which takes you back up into Burpham.*

Walk 13

# BARCOMBE MILLS AND THE RIVER OUSE

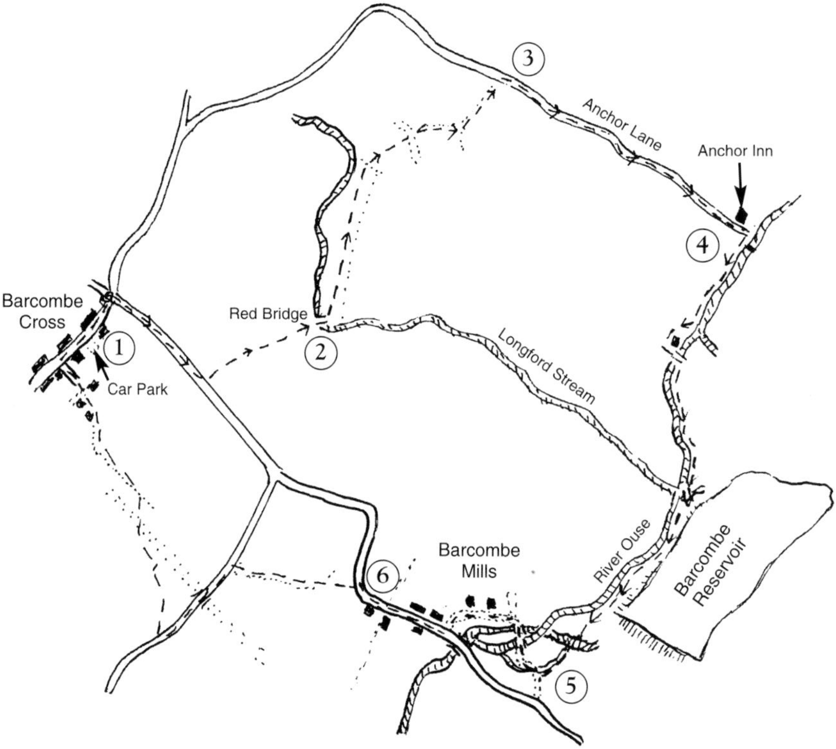

# Walk 13
# BARCOMBE MILLS AND THE RIVER OUSE

**Distance:** 4½ miles.

**Route:** Barcombe – Red Bridge – Anchor Inn – Barcombe Mills – Barcombe.

**Map:** OS Explorer 122: South Downs Way – Steyning to Newhaven.

**Start/Parking:** at the village of Barcombe, called Barcombe Cross on OS maps. Access to the village is via unclassified roads from the A275 Lewes-to-Chailey road about three miles north of Lewes. Park in the small village car park, signposted from the High Street next to the village PO/Stores at GR 420158.

**Public Transport:** occasional weekday bus from Lewes to Barcombe Cross (approximately two-hourly).

**Conditions:** good walking along field paths and the grassy river bank of the River Ouse. One short path may be ploughed out. Half a mile of quiet lane. Much of the walk is at risk of winter flooding.

**Refreshments:** Royal Oak pub at Barcombe Cross, Anchor Inn at point 4. (NB: the Angler's Rest pub at Barcombe Mills has closed down.)

Opportunities for good quality riverside walking in Sussex are rare. The lower reaches of the main Sussex rivers, although accessible on foot, have often been so dredged, re-aligned and banked up with high flood barriers as to lose their naturalness and appeal. Further upstream there are few public footpaths along river banks with one or two notable exceptions, including the delightful meandering section of river bank to the north of Barcombe Mills featured on this walk and fully deserving a special place in a book such as this one.

As a bonus, at the time of writing, you can, during the summer months, extend your exploration of the river by hiring a rowing boat from the Anchor Inn at point 4.

# THE WALK

*From the entrance to the car park* **(1)** *turn right along the High Street. At a mini-roundabout go right again, signposted to Barcombe Mills and Ringmer. About 100 yards after passing the speed de-restriction signs at the edge of the village, turn left over a stile beside a gate and follow a headland path gently downhill along the right edge of two fields. Go ahead across a low-lying meadow to cross a substantial footbridge* **(2)**, *marked as Red Bridge on the Explorer Map.*

*Beyond the bridge turn left to a stile and maintain direction through a long thin meadow bounded by a fence to the right and a meandering stream to the left. At the other end of this meadow go over a stile and bear half right up across a field where the path may be obliterated by ploughing. Aim just to the right of a prominent power pole where you will find a stile. Cross a drive and continue over a stile, almost opposite, to the left of the aforementioned pole.*

*Go forward along a left field edge to another stile and then bear half left with a hedge on your left which you can now follow to join Anchor Lane over a third stile* **(3)**. *Turn right and follow this quiet narrow lane until it ends at the Anchor Inn and the River Ouse.*

Apart from the risk of winter flooding, The Anchor Inn is perfectly situated, remote and isolated beside the river. It has recently come under new management and is a hive of activity during summer weekends

*River Ouse, Anchor Inn in background.*

*Just short of the wide bridge over the Ouse* **(4)**, *turn right and follow the right bank of the river downstream, passing massive sluice gates on your left and continuing along the grassy river bank. After about 300 yards the path diverges from the river to skirt to the right of a white weather boarded house and garden. Join the drive from this house and bear right along it. Just past a large storage barn, go left across a concrete bridge over the Ouse and turn right to continue downstream, now on the left bank of the river.*

*After just under a quarter of a mile, cross a footbridge over a side stream and continue beside the main river on your right, soon with the raised dam of Balcombe Reservoir away to your left. At the far end of the reservoir, cross a sluice, go through a swing gate and follow a more open section of the river bank. After another bridge over a feeder stream a clear path continues out to join a drive* **(5)**. *Turn right and follow this drive as it crosses a series of waterways, pools, weirs and sluices.*

This is the site of the old Barcombe Mills. The first ivy-covered bridge is Pike's Bridge across the disused canal which once allowed horse drawn barges to bypass the mill and the weirs on the main stream. There were once two locks, above and below the bridge. A second bridge crosses the head of a large trout pool beyond which a grass mound stands on the site of the flour mill which once thrived here. It was subsequently converted to a button factory but burnt down in 1939. A tiny toll house remains. A final bridge crosses the main stream of the Ouse. Several weirs and sluices are visible from the track. Note the fish ladders built into the weirs, allowing sea trout to proceed upstream.

*At a junction of tracks just past the old toll house, turn left and follow another drive to join the main road and bear right along it. Pass, on the left, the site of the old Barcombe Mills Station, and carry on past the old Angler's Rest pub, now sadly closed down.*

*After another 100 yards or so, go left over a stile* **(6)**. *You now have a choice of waymarked paths. You should aim for a stile on the skyline (not along the left field edge). Beyond the stile, maintain direction, now with a fence on your left, to join a lane over a stile. Turn left through a dip, then up and over a brick bridge across the disused railway line. About 100 yards beyond the bridge, turn right over a stile and bear slightly right across a field to the next stile, to the right of a sturdy old oak tree.*

*Continue without changing direction across a field corner to another stile, then walk round the right edge of the field beyond until, after about 150 yards you can go right over another stile and drop down to cross the line of the old railway in a wooded dip. Beyond a wooden swing gate bear left walking parallel to the fence at first, then diverging gradually from it to climb up an uneven grassy slope, passing obliquely under power lines.*

*Go over a stile in the fence on your right and forward along a good headland path which continues as a twitten which squeezes between houses and gardens. Shortly, ignore a path to the left. At a road bear left, go straight over a crossroads and along the lane ahead which takes you out to Barcombe High Street next to the Royal Oak pub. Turn right back to the start.*

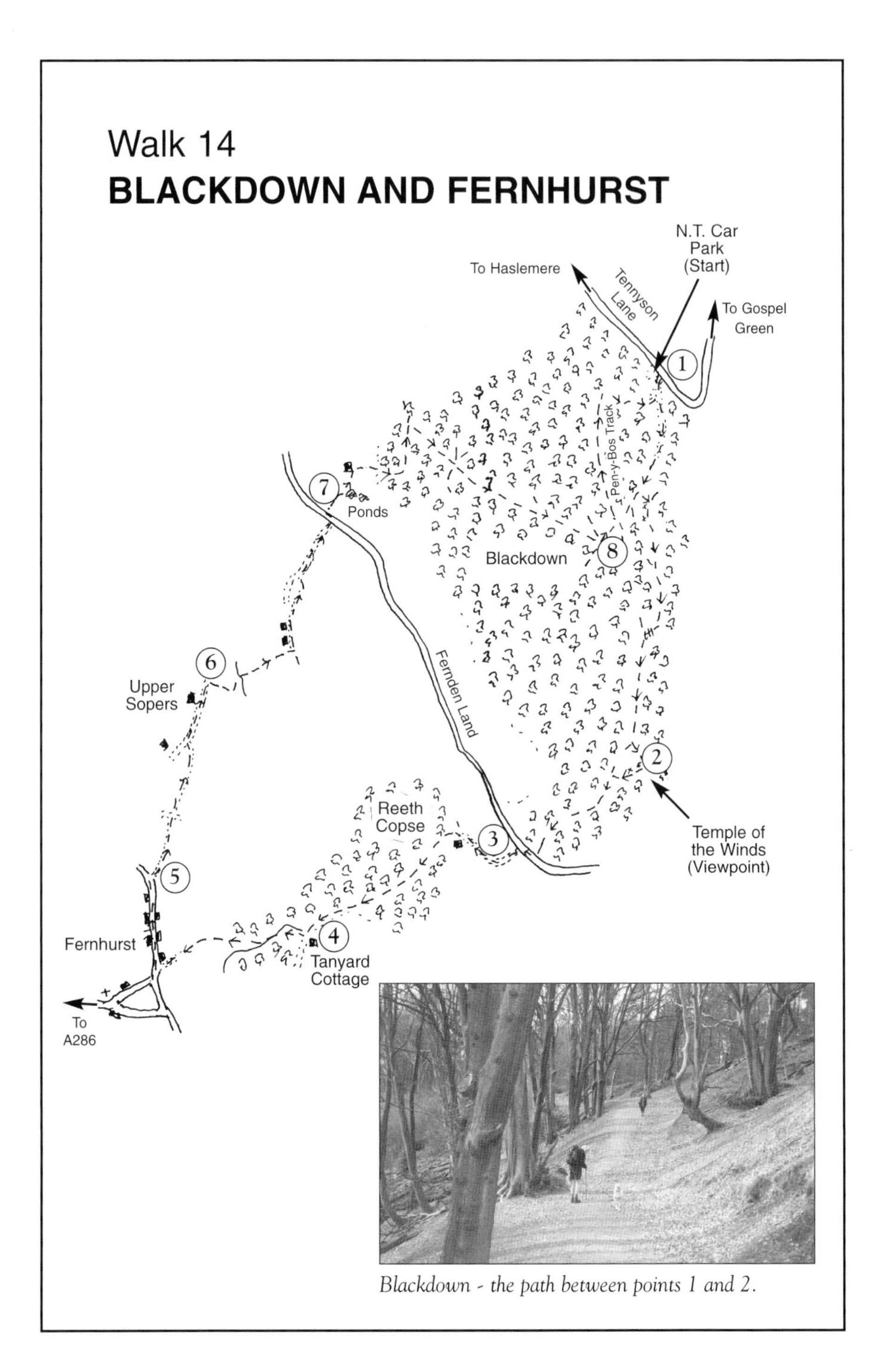


*Blackdown - the path between points 1 and 2.*

# Walk 14
# BLACKDOWN AND FERNHURST

| | |
|---|---|
| **Distance:** | $5^1/_4$ miles. |
| **Route:** | Blackdown National Trust Car Park – Temple of the Winds – Reeth Copse – Fernhurst – Upper Sopers – Blackdown. |
| **Map:** | OS Explorer 133: Haslemere and Petersfield. |
| **Start/Parking:** | from the B2131 road about a quarter of a mile east of Haslemere, follow a narrow unclassified road southwards, signposted to Blackdown and Whitwell Hatch. At two subsequent road junctions follow the signed Tennyson Lane. Park in the National Trust car park on the right of the lane at GR 920308. |
| **Public Transport:** | none convenient. |
| **Conditions:** | much of the walk is on woodland paths, some of which may be muddy after rain. One fairly stiff climb back up on to Blackdown. |
| **Refreshments:** | Red Lion pub at Fernhurst. |

No book of this kind would be complete without a walk to the highest point in Sussex. The trig point which marks the actual 918-ft summit of Blackdown is a disappointing spot, hidden away in woodland. But less than half a mile away and passed on the walk is the spectacular viewpoint known as the Temple of the Winds. The whole of the 600-acre area of Blackdown is owned and managed by the National Trust who are currently much involved in the grubbing up of the rhododendron thicket which was threatening to take over the area. Armed with a sketch map usually available from a National Trust dispenser on the back of a notice near the start of the walk, you may like to explore some of the many paths which criss-cross the area. This map could also come in useful if you do happen to stray from the described route.

From the Temple of the Winds the walk drops down to visit the pleasant village of Fernhurst where there is a convenient pub. The return route to the top of Blackdown involves a 500-ft climb but is generally well graded and fairly painless if you take your time. And this is certainly a walk to take gently and savour to the full.

# THE WALK

*Start the walk along a hard track which leaves the road next to the car park beside a National Trust notice 'Blackdown'* **(1)**. *Pass to the left of another car parking area, and go forward past low metal posts and along a wide track. Shortly join and go ahead along the signed Sussex Border Path on a sandy track between low banks.*

*After another 100 yards or so turn left along a narrow path marked with a yellow arrow indicating that it is a permissive National Trust path. Pass to the right of a seat where a superb view opens up eastwards and southwards across a wide expanse of the Weald. Beyond the seat, bear half-right dropping down for a few yards to join a track coming up the hill from the left. Bear right along this track passing in front of another seat. Keep left here on a path which is narrow at first but soon widens out.*

*Go ahead on a fine terraced track which contours along the upper slope of a beech hangar. Join a higher track up a short flight of steps and turn left. After a few yards, where you have a choice of two signposted bridleways, keep right.*

The summit trig point marking the highest point in Sussex is hidden away in the trees to the right, but is hardly worth a detour since it offers no views.

*Continue along the main track after 300 yards forking left out to the Temple of the Winds where there is a recently refurbished stone seat* **(2)**.

Pause here to enjoy what is arguably one of the finest views in Sussex, if not the south east of England. It embraces a vast Wealden panorama backed by the distant line of the South Downs. On a clear day you should be able to pick out landmarks such as Chanctonbury Ring, the masts on Bignor Hill, the Arun gap and further east the promontory of Wolstonbury Hill to the north of Brighton. Nearer at hand is Bexley Hill crowned by another prominent radio mast.

*The path through Reeth Copse between points 3 and 4.*

*Carry on past the stone seat and along a narrow winding path which passes another seat, this time wooden and rustic. Just past this seat, fork left at a Y-junction on a path which follows the edge of the steep wooded slope at first before dropping steadily down, soon entering a hollow way between wooded banks. Follow it down to join a lane and turn right.*

*After 20 yards* **(3)** *go left along a metalled drive, signposted as a public bridleway. Where the drive ends at a house and you have a choice of two tracks* *ahead, fork left, soon on another descending sunken path which tends to double as a stream. Go ahead over two crossing tracks, descending steadily.*

*Just short of the point where the path joins a concrete drive at Tanyard Cottage* **(4)**, *turn right on a delightful path which follows a stream through woodland, a good place for bluebells in the Spring. Follow this path past a recreation ground and out via an access drive to Fernhurst where you will join a road beside the Red Lion pub.*

Fernhurst is a pleasant village, particularly to the east of the main A286 road where the church, mostly the product of extensive Victorian restoration but containing some Norman fragments, and the welcoming pub are nicely placed beside the small triangular village green.

*Turn right past the pub and along the road. Where the road bends squarely round to the left* **(5)**, *you should go right along a metalled drive, signposted as a public footpath. After a few yards, where the drive ends, go ahead on an enclosed path which soon skirts round the left edge of a paddock. Cross a drive and go forward along the right edge of two fields with good views across the valley to your right to the wooded summit of Blackdown.*

*Join a lane and bear right along it. Soon after passing a large house on your left at Upper Sopers, the lane becomes a gravel track. After less than 100 yards* **(6)** *go right over a stile beside a gate and follow an unmade track down through a valley and up the other side.*

*After a 200 yard climb, where a track goes off to the left to a house, you should bear right for 20 yards, then left up a bank to a T-junction with a waymarked bridleway where you should turn left. After about 250 yards, fork left down to join a metalled drive and bear right, uphill, along it. At a junction with a lane, turn left and, after 40 yards* **(7)**, *go right along a woodland path.*

You will pass, on your right, a group of small ponds, all that remains of a string of hammer ponds, once in industrial use in connection with the iron-smelting industry which flourished in the area.

*A fenced path skirts to the right of a new house and feeds into a path which climbs steadily up the wooded western slope of Blackdown. Beyond a National Trust notice the path climbs between high banks, shored up in places by the remains of an old stone wall. At a path junction turn sharply back to the right, still climbing.*

*At another junction, at a point where the path begins to level out, bear right. Go straight over a crossing bridleway and continue very gently up with a clear felled area to your left. Ignore a track going back to the left and, at another junction of tracks* **(8)** *turn squarely left, signed as the Sussex Border Path (not sharply left down the valley). After about 100 yards, turn left along a sunken path, marked on the map as the Pen-y-Bos Track, a Celtic name indicating the ancient origins of both the path and the settlements which once occupied the area.*

*The track follows a fairly level course with a more open area to your right. Where the banks beside the sunken path finally open out, turn right on a well-trodden path which winds through woodland. At a path junction turn left for a few yards to reach the car park passed soon after the start of the walk. Turn left along the track from the car park for the short distance back to the start.*

Walk 15

# THE MENS AND FITTLEWORTH WOOD

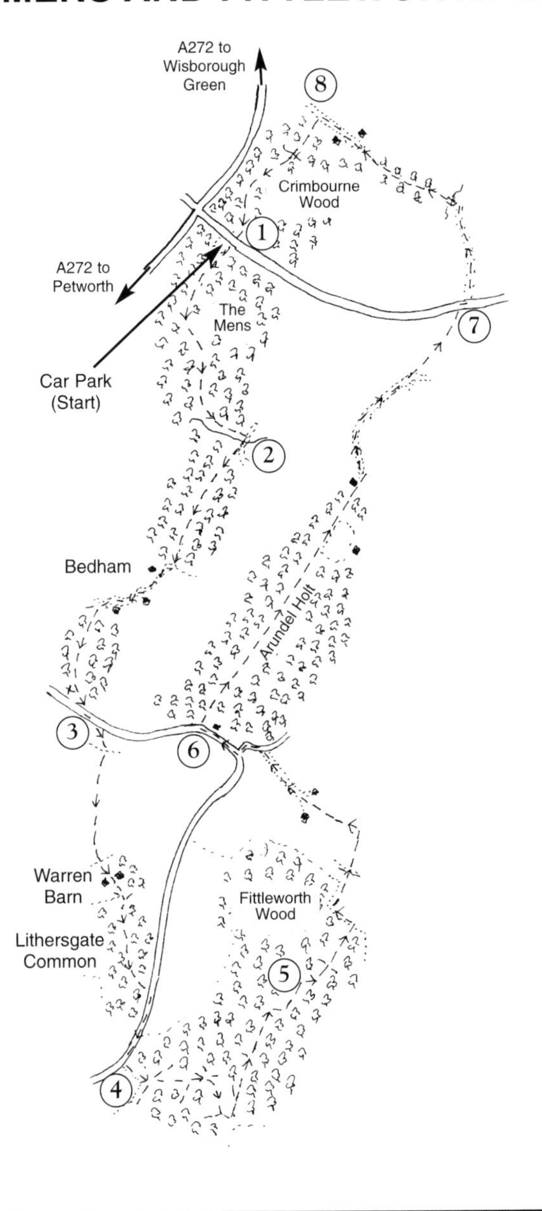

# Walk 15
# THE MENS AND FITTLEWORTH WOOD

| | |
|---|---|
| **Distance:** | $6^1/_2$ miles. |
| **Route:** | The Mens – Bedham – Warren Barn – Lithersgate Common – Fittleworth Wood – Arundel Holt – The Mens. |
| **Map:** | OS Explorer 134 - Crawley and Horsham. |
| **Start/Parking:** | in the small Mens Nature Reserve car park. It can be found about 100 yards along a narrow unclassified road which heads south eastwards from a cross roads on the A272 Petworth-to-Billingshurst road about three miles south west of Wisborough Green. The car park is to the south of the road at GR 023237. |
| **Public Transport:** | there is a bus service along the A272 if you can persuade the driver to stop at the cross roads. |
| **Conditions:** | most of the walk is on woodland paths, some shared between pedestrians and equestrians and therefore likely to be muddy after rain in spite of the well drained sandy soil. |
| **Refreshments:** | none. |

It comes as quite a surprise to discover that West Sussex is one of the most heavily wooded counties in England. So no book of this kind would be complete without a walk sampling this rich and important feature. And I can't think of a better walk in the woods than this one.

It starts out through one of the largest tracts of ancient woodland in the county. The Mens (the name is derived from the Anglo-Saxon word for Common) is a 160-acre Sussex Wildlife Trust nature reserve, managed as 'wildwood'. The area, which had been not used for timber production for many years, is now deliberately left to evolve naturally even after such events as the Great Gale of 1987. The predominant tree is beech but the age of the wood results in a diversity of trees and shrubs such as oak, holly, rowan, spindle and hawthorn as well as rarer species such as the wild service tree.

Our walk starts through The Mens using a permissive nature reserve path which is not marked on OS maps. It then climbs steadily up to the top of the Bedham escarpment, before briefly leaving the shelter of the trees to cross high ground with fine views southwards to the Downs. Continuing across patchy heathland, we then enter Fittleworth Wood, an area of predominately sweet chestnut coppice and also, in season, a good place for wild daffodils, particularly along the northern edge.

The return route uses a long straight path down through Arundel Holt where the tall beech trees and the high canopy give an impression of progression along the nave of a vast cathedral.

# THE WALK

*Start the walk along a waymarked permissive bridleway which heads squarely away from the road, along the left edge of the car park* **(1)** *and into the dense woodland of the Mens. Follow this woodland path, a bit unclear in places but assisted by occasional waymarks. It passes through an area of fine beech trees. Eventually the path runs parallel to a tiny stream on your right to a junction with a metalled drive* **(2)**.

*Turn right over a bridge across the stream and, after a few yards on the drive, fork right along a signed bridleway which soon begins to climb steeply through the wood, tunnelling between holly trees which are filling the space below the high beech canopy. Go straight over a signed crossing path and after another 300 yards or so go ahead through a partially cleared area where there are several cottages, the small community of Bedham.*

*At a T-junction, go right along a hard track. Just past a large timber fronted house on the left, fork right with the bridleway, cross a gravel track and after another 100 yards, where the bridleway divides, fork left to climb steeply up through Bedham Woods.*

Towards the top of the hill you will pass Bedham Church. Built in 1880 by a local benefactor, it has been disused and totally neglected in recent years and is now no more than a roofless shell.

*Follow the path up to a road* **(3)** *and turn left.*

Through gaps in the trees to your left you get a series of glimpses of a fine view northwards towards Hascombe Hill, the Surrey greensand ridge and the North Downs.

*Just past a post box on the right, fork right up through trees to a stile and then head slightly left across a large field where a path is usually trodden out through any growing crop.*

From this field, the only treeless area on the entire walk, a fine panorama of the South Downs opens out ahead with the masts on Bignor Hill a distinguishing landmark and the lower ground of the Arun gap almost directly ahead.

*Ignoring a signed path off to the left in the middle of the field, continue downhill to a stile and through scrub to a bridle gate. Join a drive and pass between the buildings at Warren Barn and to the right of the farm house to a stile. A path now winds up through patchy heath and woodland. Ignore a path going back to the right and, after about 10 yards, at another path junction, turn right. A good path now winds across Lithersgate Common to join a lane where you should turn right.*

*Fittleworth Wood.*

*After about 250 yards* **(4)** *go left through a gap beside a double gate. You have a choice of tracks here; keep to the one on the left which goes ahead soon entering Fittleworth Wood. Go straight over a crossing track, ignore a track to the right and, very soon, bear half right with the main signposted bridleway.*

*At a T-junction, bear left and, after 60 yards, at a second T-junction, turn left again, still on a wide track which heads north through the main bulk of Fittleworth Wood. Where you have a choice of two parallel paths ahead, keep to the one on the right. The path climbs gradually at first. Where it levels out at another T-junction, follow signs right and, after 50 yards, left.*

*Where the track divides again at a Y-junction* **(5)** *fork right, dropping steeply downhill. Go over a crossing track and a stream in a dip and climb fairly sharply up again. At the top go over another crossing track. At the edge of the wood, go through a bridle gate and left round two sides of a field. In the second field corner go through another bridle gate and forward, dropping down through more woodland. Follow this clear track as it bears left and takes you out via a house access drive to a lane.*

*Turn left and, at a road junction, go right, signposted to Bedham and Petworth. After about 200 yards* **(6)** *turn right along a signposted footpath which takes a straight course for almost a mile down through Arundel Holt, a majestic grove of tall beech trees. Ignore all crossing tracks and paths. The path eventually goes ahead beneath power lines along the left edge of a more open area, then re-enters woodland. Cross a footbridge in a dip and, after skirting to the right of a cottage, go ahead along an access drive.*

*After about 400 yards fork left along a signed woodland path, on a fairly direct route, indistinct in places, which eventually runs close to the right hand edge of the wood out to a lane. Turn right for 20 yards before going left* **(7)** *along a clear signed bridleway. After about 400 yards, follow this bridleway round to the left, over a wide bridge. After about 400 yards join and go ahead along the access drive from a house called Freelands. Just past another house on the left ignore the first signed footpath on your left.*

*After another 100 yards or so along the drive* **(8)** *go left along another woodland path to the left, waymarked as a permissive bridleway which takes you through Crimbourne Wood, another segment of The Mens, and brings you out opposite the car park.*

# Walk 16
# ST. LEONARD'S FOREST

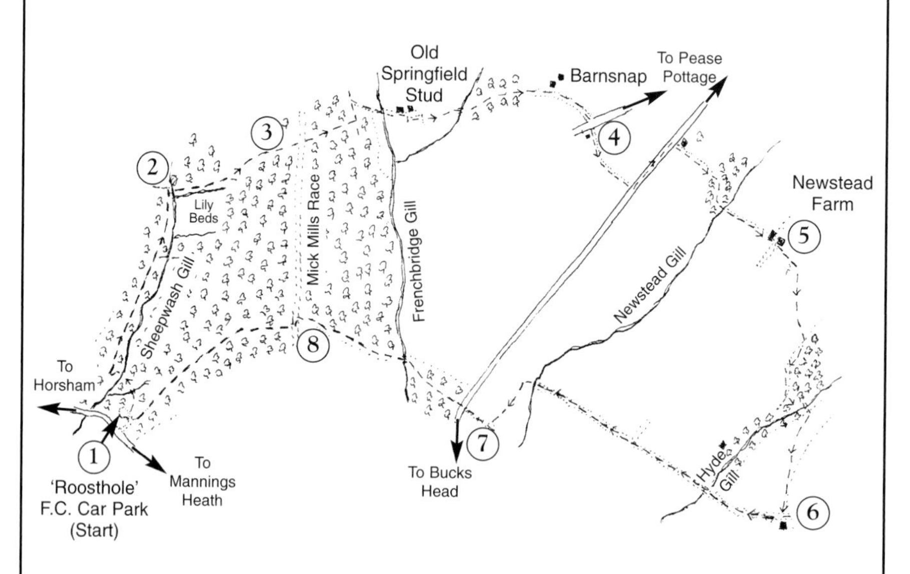

*The crossing at Sheepwash Gill.*

# Walk 16
# ST. LEONARD'S FOREST

| | |
|---|---|
| **Distance:** | $6^1/_4$ miles. |
| **Route:** | Roosthole Forestry Commission car park – Lily Beds – Barnsnap – Newstead Farm – Mick's Cross – Roosthole CP. |
| **Map:** | OS Explorer 134: Crawley and Horsham. |
| **Start/Parking:** | at the Roosthole Forestry Commission car park to the west of Horsham and to the north of Mannings Heath (GR 208298). |
| **Public Transport:** | none convenient. |
| **Conditions:** | much of the walk is along sandy forest paths and tracks, mostly well drained, though likely to be muddy in places after heavy rain. |
| **Refreshments:** | none. |

Once part of the forest of Anderida which covered the Weald, St Leonard's Forest was subsequently one of the main centres of the Wealden Iron Industry when many of the trees were felled and the hammer ponds constructed. These ponds and the occasional remains of the pits from which the iron ore was once extracted are the only remaining traces of this industrial past.

St Leonard's Forest is now part of the High Weald Area of Outstanding Natural Beauty and survives as a patchwork of mixed woodland punctuated by farmed enclaves. It is situated at the western end of a series of broken sandstone ridges which extend across the Weald between Horsham and Hastings, rising out of the Wealden clay to a local height of over 400 feet. The sandstone plateau is eroded by a series of valleys carved by tiny streams or gills and our walk traverses a cross-section of this striking landscape, following an undulating route across high ground and dropping down to cross and re-cross three of these tiny wooded gills.

# THE WALK

*From the near right hand corner, just inside the entrance to the circular parking area* **(1)**, *follow a path which starts between staggered railings and drops down through woodland. Cross a footbridge over a stream and climb again. At the top of the slope, you have a choice of several minor paths which may be a little confusing. You should go more or less directly ahead soon dropping down again fairly steeply into a wider valley. Cross Sheepwash Gill in a lovely forest glade and climb again.*

*Very shortly, join a wide well worn path and turn right to head north along the side of the valley with the slope dropping away to the gill on your right. At a meeting of four ways, go directly ahead, still keeping the stream nearby on your right. Where you join a signed footpath coming in from the right over a ford, you should go directly ahead without crossing the stream.*

*After another 300 yards or so, at a T-junction* **(2)**, *turn right across an earth dam at the head of a small pond and follow a wide track up through the forest.*

You are now on part of the High Weald Landscape Trail, a recently established long distance path across the High Weald of Sussex and Kent. It starts from Horsham in the West and meanders for over 90 miles to finish at Rye to the east of Hastings, well signed and waymarked throughout.

*After about a quarter of a mile fork left along a narrower path, go straight over a crossing ride and on to reach another wide straight crossing ride* **(3)**.

*The path near point 3.*

This is known locally as Mick Mills Race. According to legend, Mick Mill, a local smuggler, raced with the Devil along this wide track on which no tree has been able to grow since.

*The Landscape Trail (which we will pick up again later in the walk) goes off to the right here along the ride but you should go straight ahead, soon dropping steeply down. At a T-junction with a track at the bottom of the slope turn left.*

*After about 100 yards, turn right along a path which drops down within the right edge of a conifer plantation. At the bottom go forward over Frenchbridge Gill and along a wide grassy track. When opposite the first of the buildings at Old Springhead Stud on your left, side-step to the right over a stile. A fenced path skirts to the right of the house and garden to another stile. Now go forward with a fence, left, to a third stile and then veer slightly right, dropping down across a field to a footbridge from which a woodland path continues.*

*Ignoring a signed path to the left go ahead, soon joining an access drive which takes you out to a road at Barnsnap. Your next path starts opposite* **(4)**, *descending between widely spaced fences at first then up again along a left field edge to join a lane. Turn left and, after 350 yards, turn right along a narrow fenced path. Follow this clear path down to cross Newstead Gill and up along a left field edge.*

*Skirt to the right of the buildings at Newstead Farm* **(5)**, *cross a metalled drive and go ahead on a track of rammed chalk. Where the track turns squarely right, you should veer half right across a field towards an electricity pylon. Once past the pylon you can head for a stile a little to the left of a corner of woodland. When inside the wood keep right, close to the edge of the wood until, after less than 200 yards, you can leave the wood again over a second stile. Follow the wood edge for a while and then re-enter the wood over a third stile.*

*Your path now descends to cross Hyde Gill. Cross another stile and bear right along the wood edge. After a few yards, where the wood edge bears right you should go ahead climbing obliquely up a grassy slope, converging on and finally joining a fence in view up the hill on your left. Follow this fence to join a drive* **(6)**.

*Turn right along the drive. This is another section of the High Weald Landscape Trail, though you are now following it in the opposite direction, back towards Horsham. Where the concrete drive turns squarely right, go ahead along an unmade track across high ground with wide views and down into the next valley. Recross Newstead Gill at a ford and, after a few yards, bear half left, up across pasture following tractor wheels. On the other side of the field turn right along a tree lined path which takes you up to join a road* **(7)**.

*Cross the road and follow the woodland path opposite, down through a valley, crossing back over Frenchbridge Gill, then up again. At the top of the hill bear left at a T-junction and, after a few yards you will come out at the southern end of Mick Mill's Race* **(8)**, *the wide ride crossed earlier in the walk at point 3. Turn left here and after a few yards fork right along a wide forest track which takes you straight back to the car park, a little over half a mile away.*

# Walk 17
# BALCOMBE AND WAKEHURST

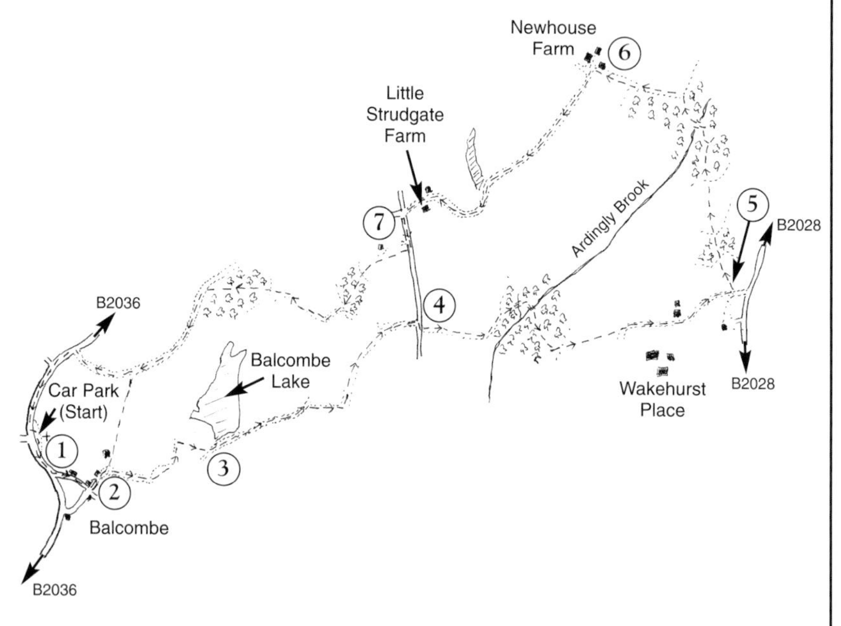

*Wakehurst Woods.*

Walk 17

# BALCOMBE AND WAKEHURST

| | |
|---|---|
| **Distance:** | $6^1/_4$ miles. |
| **Route:** | Balcombe Church – Balcombe Village – Balcombe Lake – Wakehurst – Newhouse Farm – Little Strudgate Farm – Balcombe Church. |
| **Map:** | OS Explorer 135: Ashdown Forest. |
| **Start/Parking:** | at Balcombe Church (GR 307309) where there is an extensive lay-by on the eastern side of the B2036 road to the north of Balcombe village. |
| **Public Transport:** | train to Balcombe Station, half a mile south of the start. |
| **Conditions:** | mainly along good tracks and reasonably well drained woodland paths; occasional muddy patches. |
| **Refreshments:** | Half Moon pub at Balcombe. Tea rooms and restaurant in Wakehurst Place Gardens (National Trust – entrance fee), half a mile off the main route. |

The High Weald Area of Outstanding Natural Beauty receives less attention than its similarly designated neighbour to the south, the Sussex Downs, but it is a landscape of comparable beauty which must feature strongly in any collection of the finest local walks. This circuit explores part of the Western High Weald, a landscape characterised by sandy ridges and deep valleys carved by streams forming the headwaters of the River Ouse.

From the village of Balcombe our outgoing route descends to Balcombe Lake before crossing a low ridge and dropping down again into the deeper valley of the Ardingly Brook, the main feeder of the Ardingly Reservoir to the south. We then climb through a segment of the wooded Wakehurst estate with an opportunity to extend the walk into Wakehurst Place Gardens.

# THE WALK

*From the lay-by at the start* **(1)** *head south beside the B2036 road until you can fork left along the Haywards Heath Road and walk into Balcombe village. At a road junction by the Half Moon pub* **(2)**, *turn left, passing the village stores on your left, and, after a few yards, bear right where the road becomes a roughly metalled track. Follow this track, passing through a gap to the left of a gate.*

*After another 200 yards, where the track bears right, you should go half left round the left edge of Balcombe cricket ground and on along a well trodden path through an area of scrub to a kissing gate leading out into a field corner with a fine view ahead across a wooded valley.*

*You have a choice of signed paths here. Keep left along the left field edge. After 100 yards or so turn squarely right and drop downhill. At the bottom go over a plank bridge through a kissing gate and bear half left across a field to a similar gate* **(3)**. *Go ahead along a track on top of the dam at the head of Balcombe Lake. Follow this drive up out of the valley until, after about 400 yards, you can turn right over a stile beside a gate and walk along a left field edge. In the field corner go left over a stile beside a gate and head squarely out across a field, aiming a little to the right of a prominent barn. In the far right field corner cross another stile and go forward along a headland track with a high hedge on your right. In the next field corner go over a stile and ahead on a gravel drive out to a lane* **(4)**.

*Turn right and, after 15 yards, left over a stile. A path now drops down into the next valley along a right field edge with the woodlands of Wakehurst in view directly ahead. Follow this field edge down and round to the left until you can go through a bridle gate. A woodland path descends to cross the Ardingly Brook, then up and down to a second stream crossing. The path is now carefully signed as it climbs, passing through a deer fence and across a segment of Wakehurst Place Gardens before continuing up across a field, squeezed between high deer fences.*

*Join and go ahead along a drive, soon passing, on the left, some new buildings which house a national seed bank, a Millennium Fund project. Continue along this drive or a parallel path until you are about 60 yards short of the B2028 road* **(5)**. *To visit Wakehurst Gardens, carry on out to the road, turn right and right again through the car park to the main entrance.*

Wakehurst Place Gardens are jointly managed by the National Trust and the Royal Botanic Gardens, Kew. They incorporate ornamental areas and extensive woodlands with several miles of laid out woodland walks. They are open every day except Christmas and New Years Day (10 to 7 in summer, shorter hours in winter).

*To continue the walk, turn left at point 5 through a gate in a deer fence and follow an unfenced grassy strip across a field. Beyond another gate continue with a deer fence on your left. Beyond a third gate and stile the path heads out across a large field, without changing direction, to a stile.*

*A path now drops down through woodland, steep in places. Shortly, join and go ahead along a wider, fairly level, track. At a signed path junction turn left and descend to recross*

*Pond near Newhouse Farm.*

*the Ardingly Brook and climb again on a rocky uneven path. Leave the wood over a stile and follow a left field edge. In the field corner go over a stile beside a gate and forward along a right field edge to join a drive near Newhouse Farm* **(6)**.

*Turn left and follow this drive down through a wooded dip with an attractive lake on the right and up again, passing Little Strudgate Farm to join a lane opposite a junction* **(7)**.

*Turn left along Paddockhurst Lane. After about 250 yards turn right over a stile beside a gate and go ahead skirting to the left of a cottage garden before veering slightly left across a field to enter woodland over a stile. Now follow a wide path through this mixture of fine mature oak and beech interspersed with new planting. At a path junction on the other side of the wood, turn right along a path, enclosed at first. After 100 yards, where the path opens out, go ahead through a gateway and ahead along a left field edge. Watch out for an area of soft mud just past the gate.*

*After about 60 yards go directly ahead across the field, now diverging from the field edge and passing a little to the right of a power pole. At a fingerpost veer left, passing beside several giant oak trees to find a stile into woodland, from which a path descends through the wood.*

*At the bottom of the hill, cross a sleeper causeway and, after a few yards join a track and go left over a substantial stone bridge, ignoring a signed path to the right just past the bridge. You can now follow this track for half a mile out to the B2036. If in need of refreshment, look out for a signed path to the left which leads back up to Balcombe village and the Half Moon. For the shortest route back to the start, follow the drive to the B2036 and turn left back to the start.*

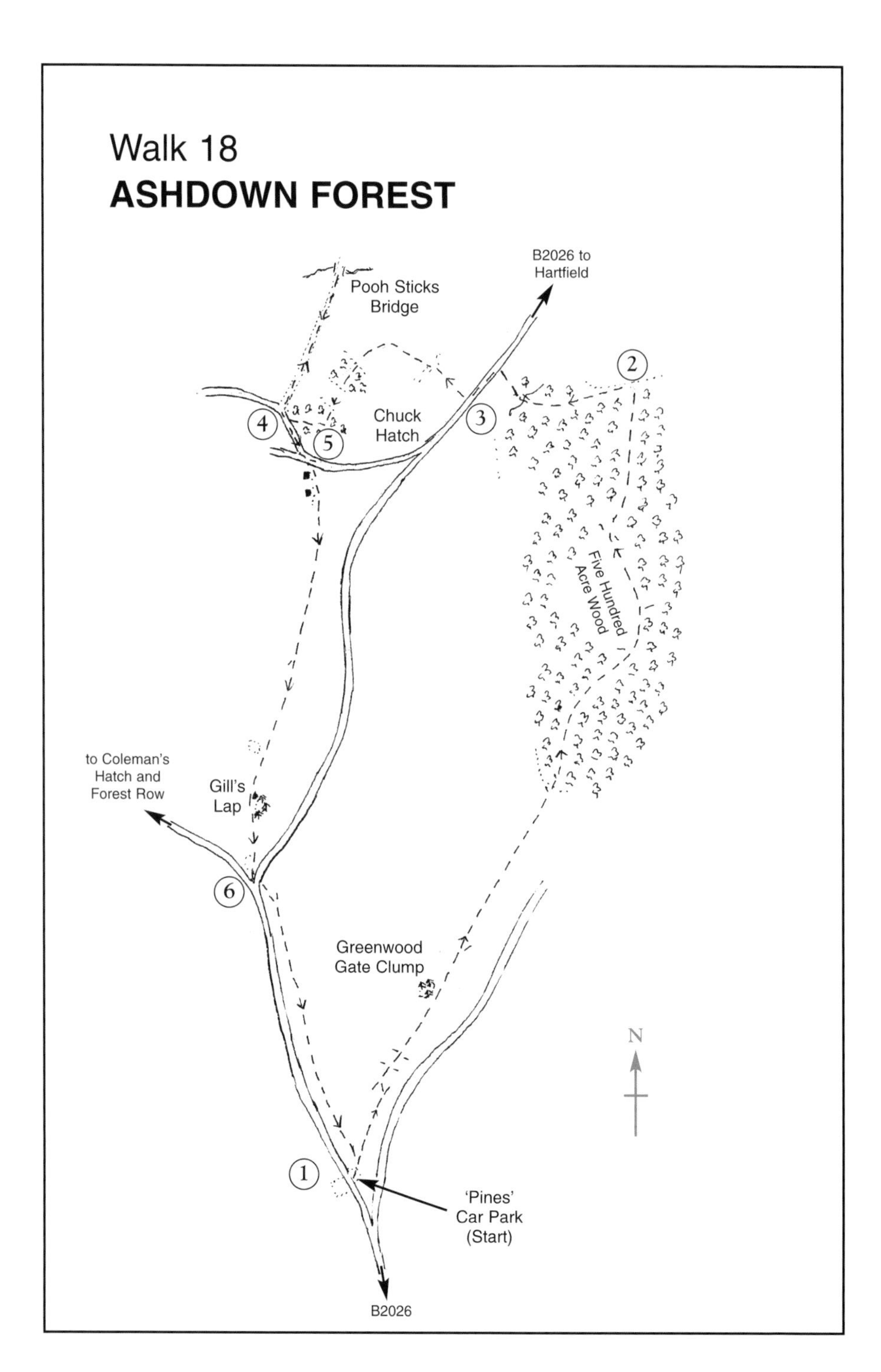
Walk 18
ASHDOWN FOREST
B2026 to
Hartfield
Pooh Sticks
Bridge
2
Chuck
Hatch
3
4
5
Five Hundred
Acre Wood
to Coleman's
Hatch and
Forest Row
Gill's
Lap
6
Greenwood
Gate Clump
N
1
'Pines'
Car Park
(Start)
B2026

Walk 18

# ASHDOWN FOREST

| | |
|---|---|
| **Distance:** | 5 1/2 miles (6 1/4 miles including extension to Pooh Sticks Bridge). |
| **Route:** | King's Standing – Greenwood Gate Clump – Five Hundred Acre Wood – (extension to Pooh Sticks Bridge) – Chuck Hatch - Gill's Lap – King's Standing. |
| **Map:** | OS Explorer 135 – Ashdown Forest. |
| **Start/Parking:** | at King's Standing on the top of the Forest. Park in the forest car park labelled 'Bushy Willows', to the left (west) of the B2026 road about 100 yards north of its junction with the B2188 road at GR 472302. |
| **Public Transport:** | none convenient. |
| **Conditions:** | much of the walk follows sandy tracks and paths, usually well drained but occasionally muddy. One steady climb up to Gill's Lap. |
| **Refreshments:** | none. |

Ashdown Forest was first established as a Royal Hunting Ground in the 13th Century. Originally 14,000 acres, it was partially enclosed in the 17th century. The 6400 acres of surviving heath and woodland are still the largest expanse of open country in southeast England. The whole area is now owned by East Sussex County Council and managed by a Board of Conservators. The public have right of access on foot over the Forest with a choice of over 100 miles of paths, rides and firebreaks. The boundaries of the open access area are now usefully marked on the latest edition of the Explorer Map.

Our walk starts at King's Standing on the top of the forest, so named because it was probably the site of a royal shooting box used by Henry VIII and James I. After passing Greenwood Gate, the highest point on the Forest, we drop down through Five Hundred Acre Wood, an extensive area of thicker woodland. After the opportunity for an optional excursion to Pooh Sticks Bridge, a steady climb then brings us back up to Gill's Lap, an exceptional viewpoint.

# THE WALK

*From the car park entrance* **(1)**, *cross the road and walk into a small car parking area opposite. Immediately turn left along a grassy path. After 40 yards, where you have a choice of wide grassy rides, fork right (almost directly ahead), diverging at about 40 degrees from the road away to your left and heading generally northwards across open heath land.*

*After a little over a quarter of a mile, where the main ride bears away to the right, you should fork left along a narrow sandy path and, after less than 100 yards, at a T-junction with a wide grass ride, turn right. Go straight ahead over two crossing tracks, the second laid with perforated concrete.*

Shortly, on your left, you will pass Greenwood Gate Clump, largely replanted but still containing one or two older and taller Scots Pines. At 730 feet above sea level this is the highest point on Ashdown Forest, though not a particularly good viewpoint.

*Continue along the main ride, ignoring all side paths. For the next mile or so you will be following part of the Wealdway, a long distance footpath linking Eastbourne with Gravesend, marked by low wooden posts with the 'WW' logo and the direction scored in the top. About 350 yards north of the clump, ignore a left fork and, after another 50 yards, take a second left fork, marked with a Wealdway post.*

*A sandy track continues as an intermittent view opens out to the left towards the tree clump on Gill's Lap which we will be passing on the return route. Where the track divides fork left with the Wealdway and a view ahead northwards across the upper Medway valley. At another junction of tracks bear left, entering Five Hundred Acre Wood. After a few yards, at another junction, go directly ahead, ignore a descending left fork. Beyond another reassuring Wealdway post the path begins to gradually descend. Beyond a gateway go straight ahead, dropping down through planted woodland. Ignore a right fork.*

*At a T-junction at the edge of the wood* **(2)** *turn left along a sandy track with a deer fence on your right at first. Cross a stream in a delightful glade shaded by giant beech trees and after a few yards fork right uphill and out to join the B2026 where you should turn left. After about 150 yards* **(3)** *go right over a stile, cross a gallop and head half right across pasture. Follow waymarks through a gate, over a stile and across a drive to another stile. Now walk across the field to a stile in the far right corner from which a woodland path continues. Head through the wood, joining and following a post and rail fence on your right. Leave the wood through a swing gate, cross a grassy paddock between two woods, go forward for a few yards in the second wood and turn right along a path worn by thousands of tiny pilgrims on their way to Pooh Sticks Bridge. It takes you out to a lane* **(4)**.

*If you are omitting the detour to Pooh Sticks Bridge turn left here. To visit the bridge, go ahead along the lane for a few yards and turn right along a wide access track for 600 yards, returning the same way.*

Pooh Sticks Bridge, immortalised in A.A. Milne's 'House at Pooh Corner' was

The new Pooh Sticks Bridge - rebuilt 1999.

first built in1907, restored in 1979 and rebuilt once more in 1999, copying the original design. Carry your own 'pooh sticks' with you as the surrounding area has been stripped bare of any loose twigs.

*Resuming the walk, follow the lane left from point 4 to a road junction and turn left again. Ignoring the first drive, after 100 yards* **(5)** *turn right along the second drive on your right, to a house called 'Woodruff'. Skirt to the left of houses and, where the drive ends, go ahead along a path which continues as a wide rising forest track. Fork left by a seat, still climbing steadily.*

On the right of the path towards the top of the hill is a small enclave containing a commemorative plaque to A.A. Milne, author of the Christopher Robin children's stories and his illustrator E.H. Shepherd. It is a fine viewpoint for the wide view to the north.

*At the top of the hill, pass to the right of the trig point and the tree clump on Gill's Lap. This is Milnes 'enchanted place on the top of the forest' which he called Galleon's Lap. A wide track crosses level high ground with more views across the valley to the right towards Nutley and, over to the left, Greenwood Gate Clump.*

*Walk past the Gill's Lap car park* **(6)**, *cross the B2026 at its junction with the unclassified road to Coleman's Hatch and Forest Row and follow the wide track opposite which starts between low wooden posts. After 150 yards fork right with the main ride which heads generally south, parallel to the road away to the right. It takes you back after about half a mile to the start.*

Commemorative Plaque and view to the North-Gill's Lap.

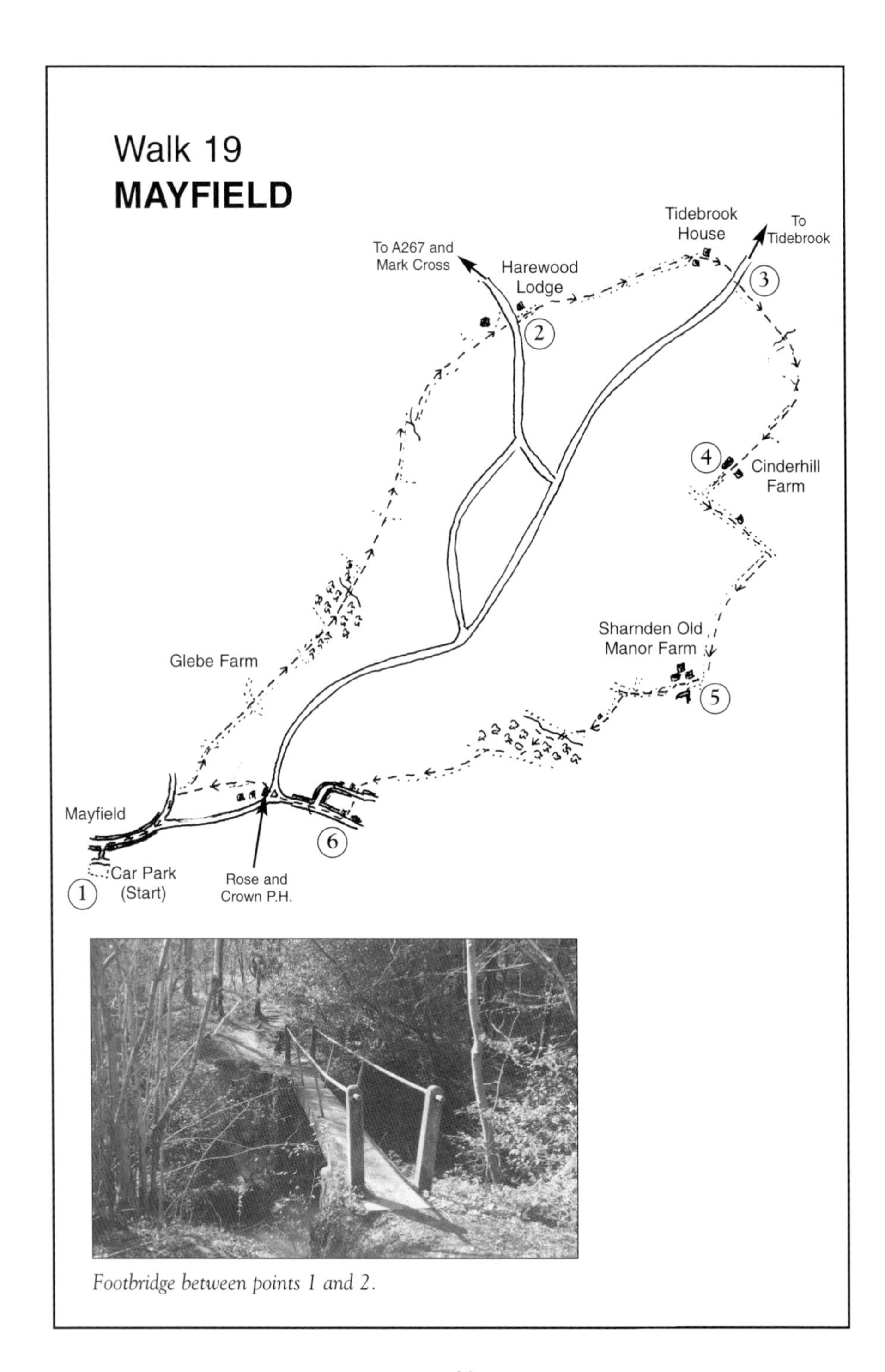


*Footbridge between points 1 and 2.*

Walk 19
# MAYFIELD

| | |
|---|---|
| **Distance:** | $5\frac{1}{2}$ miles. |
| **Route:** | Mayfield – Vicarage Wood – Harewood Lodge – Tidebrook House – Cinderhill Farm – Sharnden Old Manor Farm – Hole Wood – Mayfield. |
| **Map:** | OS Explorer 136: The Weald. |
| **Start/Parking:** | from the village of Mayfield, accessible from the A267 Heathfield-to-Tunbridge Wells road about five miles north of Heathfield. The free village car park is signposted down a narrow lane southwards from the main village street (GR 587268). |
| **Public Transport:** | hourly weekday bus service from Eastbourne or Tunbridge Wells (two-hourly on Sundays). |
| **Conditions:** | an undulating route using field and woodland paths and some long established tracks. May be muddy in places. |
| **Refreshments:** | several pubs in Mayfield. The Rose and Crown, to the east of the village, is conveniently placed near the end of the walk. |

Deep in the thinly populated High Weald of East Sussex at the upper end of the valley of the River Rother you can discover some of the best walking in the county. It is a rich landscape of high ridges and intimate well wooded valleys carved by tiny streams. Starting from the fine hill top village of Mayfield, 500 feet above sea level, this varied circuit takes an undulating route across this delightful area using several little used paths.

The relatively short walk should leave plenty of time to explore Mayfield. The village, like many in the area, owed its original prosperity to the Wealden iron-smelting industry which once flourished in the district. The church originated in the 15th century. Nearby, once stood the Old Palace of the Archbishops of Canterbury. The remains of the Palace are now incorporated into the fabric of a school. Many fine old stone and timber houses line the High Street, one of the most striking being the Middle House Inn, a half timbered building dating from 1575.

# THE WALK

*From the car park* **(1)** *return to the High Street and turn right. Follow the main road round to the left and after about 100 yards turn right through a brick gateway into the village recreation ground. Bear half left along the left edge of this grassy area and a subsequent football pitch, following wayposts indicating that you are on part of a Mayfield circular walk. Cross a drive, go over the stile opposite and drop down along the right edge of two fields. Cross another drive and continue downhill with a fence on your right.*

*Beyond a stile in the bottom right field corner, a path continues through scrub, along another right field edge and down through a wood where you should ignore paths to right and left.*

*At the bottom cross a substantial footbridge and bear right over a stile currently collapsed. Climb along a left field edge and then go ahead across two fields where a path should be trodden out. Keep to the right of a third field, until in the field corner you can bear right into a wood. A path winds through the wood descending to cross a stream via a broad but dilapidated bridge.*

*A few yards beyond the stream, at a signed path junction, turn left. Cross another tiny culverted stream, leave the wood and climb along a right field edge with the stream in a deep wooded gully to your right. Cross a wooded dip and climb steadily across grass, skirting to the right of a large landscaped garden to join a road in the top left field corner.*

*Cross the road* **(2)** *and go through the gateway to Harewood Lodge, opposite. The drive soon becomes a tree-lined path. Shortly fork right over a stile by a gate and follow a path downhill between banks. A path continues through the garden of Tidebrook House and out via the house drive to join a lane* **(3)**.

*Turn right for 10 yards, then left over a stile beside a gate and ahead across high ground with a hedge on your right and a fine view to the left across the Tidebrook valley. In the field corner go ahead over two stiles taking you through a wooded strip. Follow the direction of a waymark on the second stile across a field and over a stream.*

*Maintain direction across the corner of a field and uphill with a hedge, right. Go through a gate and keep to the right of the next field also. In the field corner veer half right through a gateway and forward with a high hedge and ditch on your right. Go through a gate and head for the picturesque converted oast houses at Cinderhill Farm, still with functioning wind vanes.*

*Pass to the right of the oast* **(4)** *and go forward along the drive from the farm. At a junction with another tarmac drive turn left. Beyond a cottage the drive becomes an unmade track. After another 300 yards or so turn right over two stiles and drop downhill, keeping to the right edge of two successive fields. At the far end of the second field go ahead along a track laid with concrete sleepers.*

*Shortly* **(5)** *turn right between the extensive complex of buildings, several derelict, at Sharnden Old Manor Farm. At a junction bear left along another track laid with sleepers.*

Cinderhill Farm, point 4.

*Ignore a signed path to the right and, after another 60 yards, turn left over a stile and drop downhill along a headland path, also surfaced with concrete. At the bottom of the hill pass to the left of a small building housing a water borehole. Go ahead to cross a stile and a footbridge and follow a narrow woodland path, beside the stream at first but soon bearing left up through the wood. (Ignore a lesser path which continues beside the stream.)*

*At another path junction fork left, still climbing, soon just inside the top edge of the wood. Leave the wood and go forward along a left field edge, following it right and left. In the field corner where you have a choice of two adjacent stiles, go over the one on the right, walk through a soggy dip and go ahead on a well trodden path across a field and then behind a row of houses and gardens. Shortly bear left between the houses, cross an estate road and continue between more houses out to a lane* **(6)**.

*Turn right. At a road junction by the Rose and Crown pub (good food and beer) turn right again. Almost immediately, just past the pub, fork left along a tarmac twitten which starts parallel and to the left of a drive, quickly bearing left behind houses and bringing you out in the corner of Mayfield recreation ground. Go ahead out to the road and turn left back into the village.*

Walk 20

# BRIGHTLING AND FULLER'S FOLLIES.

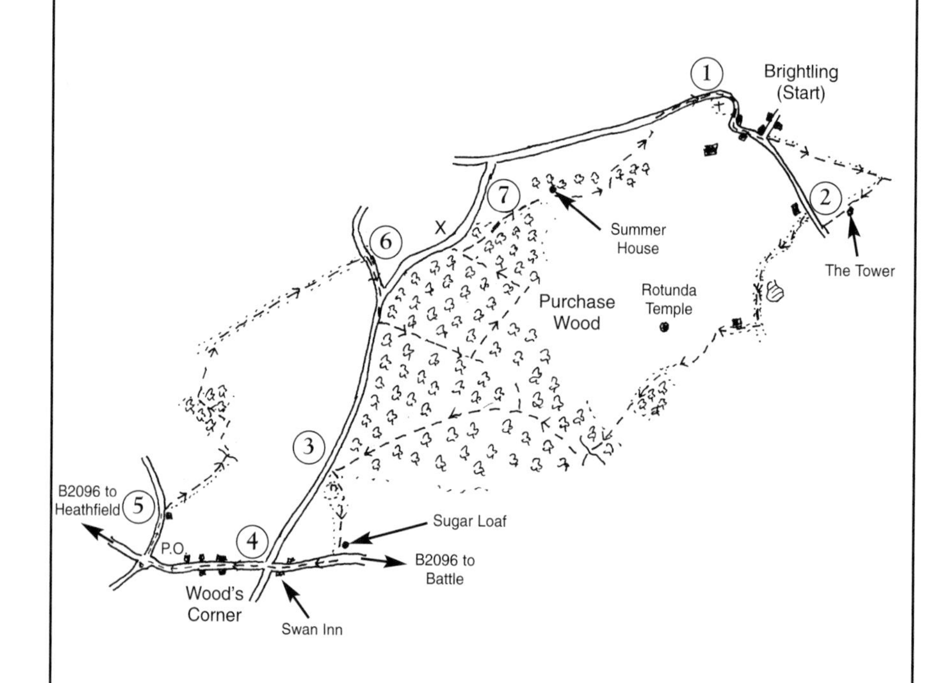

*The Pyramid.*

Walk 20

# BRIGHTLING AND FULLER'S FOLLIES.

| | |
|---|---|
| **Distance:** | $5^1/_2$ miles. |
| **Route:** | Brightling – The Tower – The Sugar Loaf – Wood's Corner – Brightling Down – Brightling Park – Brightling. |
| **Map:** | OS Explorer 124: Hastings and Bexhill. |
| **Start/Parking:** | at Brightling which is signposted from the Heathfield-to-Battle road at Wood's Corner. There is reasonable roadside parking to the west of Brightling Church alongside Brightling Park wall at GR 683210. |
| **Public Transport:** | none convenient. |
| **Conditions:** | an undulating route along field paths and woodland tracks. One short section of busy road. Be prepared for some mud after rain. |
| **Refreshments:** | Swan Inn at Wood's Corner. |

This is an attractive walk across a rolling High Wealden landscape but it owes its inclusion in this collection of special walks to the imprint of one singular man on the landscape. John ('Mad Jack') Fuller, MP, philanthropist, patron of Science and the Arts, lived at Brightling Park (then known as Rosehill) for some years after 1810, and built a number of follies, dotted around the park, most of which are visited or can be seen from this walk.

Most of the $5^1/_2$ mile circuit follows rights of way or access routes within Forestry Commission land. However, access through Brightling Park depends on a Countryside Stewardship agreement which expires in September 2013 and is therefore not assured beyond that date. The agreement may well be renewed, but if progress is barred you will have to return from point 7 to the road at point 'X' on the sketch map and follow the road (also indicated on the map) back to the start.

# THE WALK

*From Brightling Church* **(1)** *follow the road eastwards out of the village.*

You can cut across the road corner by walking through the churchyard where you will find the first of Fuller's Follies in the form of his own mausoleum, a 25 ft stone pyramid. The story once went that he was interred, dressed for dinner, sporting a top hat and seated at a table with a bottle of claret to hand. This was later disproved when the tomb was opened to carry out repairs.

*At a road junction go ahead through a swing gate between the two roads and follow a fence, left. Beyond a second swing gate, maintain direction across a field to a third swing gate and on along a sunken field edge path. Immediately beyond a fourth swing gate turn right over a stile and along a right field edge with a fine view to the left across Darwell reservoir and along the valley towards Robertsbridge and Bodiam.*

On the other side of the field is The Tower, 35 ft high, built by Fuller in 1820 allegedly so that he could overlook the progress of renovation work on Bodiam Castle which he then owned. The original internal wooden staircase, destroyed by fire, has been replaced by metal steps and a ladder allowing access to a lookout window.

*The path skirts to the right of the Tower and drops down across a field to join a lane. Turn right and, after less than 100 yards* **(2)**, *turn left along a farm track. Follow this track downhill and across a raised causeway between two ponds. After another 200 yards or so turn right along another track, signposted to the Sugar Loaf. Pass between farm buildings and after another 100 yards with the Rotunda Temple in view directly ahead turn left through a wooden gate.*

The Rotunda Temple, designed by Sir Robert Smirke, the architect of the British Museum, was built in about 1810. Fuller may have used it for gambling sessions and to entertain his guests for tea or his lady friends for less genteel purposes. Another story goes that it was used to store smuggled goods. There is no public access to the Temple.

*Follow a hedge, right, through two fields, on through a belt of woodland, and across another field to re-enter woodland. Cross a stream in a wooded dip.*

A fragment of sandstone wall on the right is part of the four-mile wall built by Fuller around the park in 1815, providing much needed work for local people at a time of poverty and high unemployment.

*At a junction with a wide sandy track turn right and after about 300 yards, at a Y-junction fork left, still on a wide forest ride. After another half a mile, just short of a road* **(3)**, *go through a stone gateway and immediately double back to the left along the access drive to an industrial site. After 40 yards fork right along an enclosed path and then up across a field to The Sugar Loaf.*

The Sugar Loaf, surely the most bizarre of Fuller's Follies, was allegedly erected in haste to win a bet that the spire of Dallington Church could be seen from his

*The Tower.*

home across the valley. It was actually lived in for a time.

*Walk out past the Sugar Loaf to the B2096 and turn right beside the road, taking care as it carries fast traffic and has no verge. Walk past the Swan Inn at Wood's Corner or, better still, drop in to sample the excellent food and the locally brewed Harvey's beer. Beyond the pub* **(4)**, *the road acquires a good pavement on the right.*

*About 400 yards past the pub, turn right along a lane, signed as a 'No Through Road'. After about 250 yards* **(5)** *go right over a stile and drop downhill with a hedge on your right. Ahead across the valley you can now see two more Follies, the 65 ft Brightling Needle on the skyline and The Observatory. At the bottom of the hill go over a culvert and stile and turn left round two sides of a field until you can go left through a wide gap in the hedge on your left next to a massive oak tree.*

*Keep to the right edge of two fields, then go forward through a hole in a hedge and on through a wood. Leave the wood through a gate and bear slightly right across pasture. Go over a stile beside a three-arm footpath sign and bear right along a tarmac drive which you should follow out to a road.* **(6)**.

*Turn right and at a road junction go right again. After 150 yards go left past a barrier into woodland where there is a Forestry Commission notice 'Deer Park'. After a little over 200 yards turn left along a broad ride and, after another 300 yards or so, at a waypost, go left again. About 50 yards short of the road, turn right.*

A detour out to the road and back provides a good view of Fuller's Observatory, another building designed by Sir Robert Smirke and completed in 1818. It was once furnished with state-of-the-art astronomical equipment and a camera obscura but is now a private residence.

*About 400 yards short of a major junction of three wide tracks, turn left at a waypost to follow a narrow woodland path. After 250 yards* **(7)**, *leave the wood through a kissing gate and bear right along a right field edge. Go through a farm gate and forward with a fence on your right. After a few yards the path opens out on to open parkland with a fine view southwards and both Rotunda Temple and Sugar Loaf in sight. Go ahead for 10 yards before turning left and immediately right, with a ditch on your right.*

On your left, after a few yards, is the last of the Follies visited on the walk, the Summer House with views over the park. It is of particular interest as it is constructed from an artificial stone called Coadestone, much used for statuary and as a building material in the early 19th Century.

*Follow the ditch until you can turn left on a broad track which takes you through a belt of woodland. On the other side of the wood bear half right across grass to a gate in the high park wall. Bear right along the road back into Brightling.*

*The Sugar Loaf.*

*The Summer House.*

# ABOUT THE AUTHOR

**Ben Perkins** was born in the village of Rodmell, near Lewes and has lived, worked and walked in Sussex throughout his life. He is a keen conservationist and long standing member of the Society of Sussex Downsmen, Society of Sussex Wealdmen and the Ramblers' Association. Over the last 15 years he has contributed more than 400 walk descriptions to a regular column in the Brighton Evening Argus and, during that time has managed to explore much of the 2000 mile network of local footpaths and bridleways.